THE
CENTURY
SPEAKS

CLEVELAND
voices

Florence Ward (*née* Gill), of Newport, Middlesbrough, in the Land Army during the First World War. (Bert Ward)

THE
CENTURY
SPEAKS

CLEVELAND
voices

Memories of Teesside, Durham, and North Yorkshire people

compiled by Neil Gander

for the **BBC Radio Cleveland** *series*
The Century Speaks

TEMPUS

First published 1999
Copyright © BBC Radio Cleveland, 1999

Tempus Publishing Limited
The Mill, Brimscombe Port,
Stroud, Gloucestershire, GL5 2QG

ISBN 0 7524 1844 0

Typesetting and origination by
Tempus Publishing Limited
Printed in Great Britain by
Midway Clark Printing, Wiltshire

For Kathryn

A school trip to Pontop Pike, *c.* 1937. Interviewee Ron Hick, from Darlington, is pictured wearing a cap. (Ron Hick)

CONTENTS

Steelworkers at Skinningrove Iron and Steel Company. (Brenda Horness)

INTRODUCTION

Gathered together in this book are some of the highlights of sixteen programmes broadcast on BBC Radio Cleveland in the autumn of 1999, under the title *The Century Speaks*. The series itself was a distillation of about 300 hours of interviews recorded throughout (what was) Cleveland, south and west Durham and North Yorkshire between November 1998 and March 1999.

The Century Speaks is a joint venture between the BBC and the British Library, to create a permanent record of everyday life in the twentieth century. We tried to collect, not only memories of life as it used to be, but reflections on how things are as the century draws to a close. We hope it will prove an invaluable resource for future historians. Imagine if the Victorians or even Mediaeval people had had access to digital recording technology!

Readers may be surprised to find little about coal mining, steel working or the other traditional industries of the region. This is because the British Library felt it had a wealth of such material already. Instead, we concentrated on areas of people's domestic and personal lives – housing, money, food, families, health, leisure and the impact of technology, to cite but a few examples. However, it was a surprise to me how few people now have a direct connection with heavy industry, although their parents or grandparents may well have worked in them.

Loftus Senior School Shinty Team, 1938. From left to right, back row: Vi Pritchard, Joyce Oglesby, Dot Cuthbert, Margery Gibson, Kathleen Watson. Front row: Iris Marks, Grace Oglesby, Nancy Watson, Brenda Horness (née Varty), Mildred Verrill, Irene Wood. (Brenda Horness)

In this book we've concentrated mainly on the 'memories' aspect of the interviews because these will be most interesting to contemporary readers. Future generations might find the details of day-to-day 'modern' life just as interesting when they delve into the British Library archive 100 years from now.

Most of the photographs are from the attics, cupboards and albums of people interviewed for *The Century Speaks*. Some subjects, however, proved more difficult than others to illustrate. 'Making ends meet' is a good example as photography was always an expensive hobby.

All the interviews will reside at the British Library in London. The Millennium Memory Bank, as it will be known, contains these and thousands more interviews from our sister BBC local and regional radio stations around the UK. The archive is also open to the general public, by arrangement with the British Library. If you wish to take advantage of the service, contact the National Sound Archive enquiry line on 0171 412 7440, or write to:

Oral History,
British Library National Sound Archive,
96 Euston Road,
London NW1 2DB

ACKNOWLEDGEMENTS

Judy Tait performed a magnificent job in research for *The Century Speaks* and in tracking down photographs for this book.

Arnold Miller gave much valuable advice during the editing of the radio programmes on which this book is based.

David Peel and the staff at BBC Radio Cleveland made life far easier than I deserved.

The staff at Beamish North of England Open Air Museum in Co. Durham were an enormous help in filling some of the photographic gaps in the book.

Araf Chohan gave me generous access to his huge collection of old postcards and photographs as well as the Chohan family archives.

Tiffany Reed at Tempus Publishing Limited has given unfailing support.

Finally, I would like to thank everybody who gave so freely of their time, tea and cake during the recording of the interviews and who entrusted me with their photographs, many of which are valued family records.

CHAPTER 1

Town and country

The places where we live are more than bricks and mortar, hills or valleys. They are also about people, communities, occasions and changes. We soon found that people found it quite hard to express their feelings about these while sitting in an armchair in their living rooms. So we decided to go 'on location'.

North Skelton village football team victory parade, 1953/54 season. They won five trophies. (Colin Berwick)

Changes

I lived in Hartlepool before the war for four years when my father came here to be an insurance agent. Then the war started and dad went away to the RAF and my grandparents insisted that mother and myself and my baby brother went to live with them. So I went to live in a mining village for five years and I came back here when I was thirteen.

I'd started secondary school while I was in Durham, and I came back and started the girls' high school here. I stayed here until I was married at the age of twenty-two.

We're standing in Colwyn Road which is the road I used to go up and down every day when I worked at ICI because I had to catch the bus on the corner there where the big roundabout is now. We're actually standing on some of the old cobbles – the whole road was

like this. They're made from slag. They're obviously very hard wearing. They've been there at least sixty or seventy years that I know of – probably longer.

We're alongside the Burn Valley Gardens. This is one of the places I wanted to see, to see whether the tennis courts are still here and they're not. They've gone. My husband and I used to play on these courts before we were married, and obviously the gardens have changed somewhat.

You never were allowed to ride bikes through it. I don't know whether you are now – I don't suppose you are…and there's the burn that the Burn Valley is named for. I don't think this has changed much. There's better protection to stop children falling in than there was in my day. Little boys who were venturesome could just get into the beck and it wasn't a very pleasant thing and it was quite

Burn Valley Gardens, West Hartlepool, probably in the first decade of the century. (Araf Chohan)

North Skelton Sword Dancers photographed on Caleb Bland's land. (Norma Templeman)

dangerous in fact. You can see it runs into a culvert here and now it's all properly protected.

Jean Kendall, age 66
Hurworth, Darlington

For The Better?

I get very sad to see the changes that have occurred over the years, not all of them for the best.

We're now at the bottom of Bolckow Street. The first house in Bolckow Street belonged to Mrs Bland. Her husband was called Caleb. Mr Bland, his son, still lives there now. The garden opposite belongs to Mr Bland. He also had some land here. Then this was sold and became a dairy and it was a dairy until Les Bell bought it and took it over to the industrial estate. As from one week ago, all this machinery has come in here and it's now going to be eight dwellings and ten garages, or twelve.

North Skelton was the only mining village that hadn't been tampered with. Now it has. Not only at the bottom of Bolckow Street, but also further on as I'll tell you when we get there.

Norma Templeman, age 61
North Skelton

Flower Parade, North Skelton, 1910 or '11. (Norma Templeman)

Burn Valley Road

You can see these houses are quite small and you go straight into them from the street, but this is a lot better than when I lived here because parts of it have been pedestrianized and therefore they have more protection from the dirt and the noise and the traffic. Of course, there weren't as many cars and things in those days.

Then this street, which is the last one at the end of Colwyn Road, is Burn Valley Road and that's the road I lived in with my parents. We lived at number 15. There are two sorts of houses in Burn Valley Road. On one side there are the big Victorian houses and on the right hand side there are the smaller artisans' houses and we lived in one of the smaller ones. It was the first house that my father had been able to buy and

they were very, very pleased because it meant a lot to them. I think they thought it meant they'd arrived. They had their own home.

This is the house I lived in with my parents. The windows have changed downstairs, and the front door…and this is the house I was married from. You can see you walk straight in from the street and into the house. It had a tiny little sitting room at the front and a bigger everyday living room at the back and then a kitchen behind there. I can see at the top of the road, Elwick Road School. I went there, my brother went there, my sister went there. And it's still there.

Jean Kendall, age 66
Hurworth, Darlington

A Good Pint

We've now crossed over the road and arrived at what was the 'Tute. The 'Tute was really at the centre of the village but only, mainly, for miners. As you walked through the door, on your left was the room where the billiards were played… dominoes I would think…always the newspaper. Mr and Mrs Bolton were caretaker and kept it spotlessly clean. At the other side, on the right, was the cloakroom and the 'Big Room' which was used for dances and any functions at all. At one point during the war it was a restaurant. You could get a meal.

We're now at The Bull's Head which hasn't changed. It's been like this as long as I can remember. The only difference is new signs have gone up. The doorway and everything is exactly as I can remember it was. 'Course, the inside's all been changed. But otherwise it's just as it was. Even the windows are just as they were.

At that time the landlord was called 'Nimble Nat' – Mr Addison. It was a lovely pub. He had a good pint…so I'm told. And during the war there was a lady lived opposite The Bull called Ada Wilkinson. By, did she love a pint! And she would go in The Bull on that piano and she could belt anything out and

Elwick Road School football team, Hartlepool, 1925/26. (Beamish. The North of England Open Air Museum, Co. Durham)

sing at the top of her voice. And then at ten o'clock, it would come out…it would be turning-out time. And there was a seat outside the 'Tute. And on that seat would be old Floss, Edie Belrow and one or two more and they'd wait 'til turning-out time. And our Tut, Freddy Hugill and Frankie Winspear would stand and sing to them all.

Norma Templeman, age 61
North Skelton

Park Hotel

We're standing outside the Park Hotel – it's a new public house. I can remember when it was built. I can also remember my father wasn't very pleased about it being built. Park Road was one of the nicer areas of the town and it didn't need another public house in it. That was how he felt.

Jean Kendall, age 66
Hurworth, Darlington

Old Winder

Now we're coming towards a hilly piece of land that's grassed over. That was the shale heap. When the pit was all dismantled, instead of taking it away it was decided to leave it and let it grass over, which it has done – to what use, I haven't the foggiest idea! But of course, it was twice as high as that and we used to get an old board or something and – ooh – we could come down there – marvellous!

That building to my right is the old winder – the old winder house. When you had the pit there you could look up

Tom Leonard, 'Tut' Templeman, Frank Winspear and Fred Hugill in The Bull, North Skelton. (Norma Templeman)

North Skelton Prize Silver Band, 1939. (Norma Templeman)

there, you would see the pit head – you'd see the winder; but you could see through them to all the green fields and everything beyond, you see. So I'm filled with sadness. I remember – most children do – running up here, and my dad worked on t' pit top as a banksman: 'Dad, I want to go to Loftus Regal, and me mam has no money.' And he'd throw me two bob down, or he'd say, 'Run up steps!' and it was up, along and up.

Norma Templeman, age 61
North Skelton

Individuality

We're walking through the Middleton Grange Shopping Centre now. It was built after I left the town and I was used to shopping in the usual grid-iron of square streets with all the little shops along them and this is all very different. It's like a lot of indoor shopping centres in most of the towns that I've been to.

Because I'm older I miss the individual shops that we used to have and the fact that you got to know the people who owned them and they knew your likes and dislikes. You always felt as if you were part of what was happening in their shop. Now you go to those big shopping centres and they're not the same, to my mind, because it doesn't matter whether you go to the shopping centre in Hartlepool or in Stockton or in Darlington, it's the same stores that you find there. And really, I prefer a bit of individuality.

Jean Kendall, age 66
Hurworth, Darlington

A general view of West Hartlepool, probably late 1950s. The Middleton Grange Shopping Centre now occupies most of the area in the middle left of this view. (Araf Chohan)

Two Monkeys

We're walking towards, now, Richard Street…the back of the street, not the front. Down here, there's always been allotments – always. My gran and granddad came from Whitby and bought number 12 Richard. Funnily enough, my husband came from number 12. He bought it after gran went.

Opposite number 12 was my granddad's hut. He was the local joiner and they all had a yard gate or a pair of steps. It housed his two monkeys at one point. There was a big hut there and inside there was all these beautifully kept tools and wood

of any description. He loved wood. And his allotment was at the back. And inside the hut he got two monkeys, called after my mum and dad – Rox and Rene. And they loved it. It was a massive great big cage they were in but they got out and bolted the wall at the end of the allotments into old Mr Dowson's orchard. And they caused havoc! And of course, they had to be caught. Well, there was that much controversy he got shot of them.

He even had a little bed in there and a little pot on his stove. He had a few hens and was as hard as nails…and yet, when he ever needed one of those hens their neck wringing for the pot, he had to go for a lady opposite to wring its neck. He couldn't do it!

Norma Templeman, age 61
North Skelton

Big Wesley

You see all these lamp standards – these have only been put up recently. They're quite elegant aren't they? Well, before the war when I lived here they had standards like that but they were for the trolley wires, because we had trolley buses here. They used to have wires all the way along the main roads and the trolleys used to have a pole that hooked onto the wire and then they were driven by electricity. And, for instance, when they went up Grange Road to the park, there was a big turning circle there and the conductor had to unhook the pole and walk round the trolley and put it on at the other end so that it could go back down the road again. I thought it was a very clean form of transport.

If we just walk to the traffic lights we'll be able to see 'Big Wesley', the big Wesleyan Methodist church…aha! Now, I knew it hadn't been used as a church for a long time, and it's now called The Wesley. I don't know whether that means it's a night club – it looks as if it might be! But what a magnificent building. It's got almost a Greek temple frontage, and that's been cleaned up. You can see, it's lovely

A tram on Church Street, West Hartlepool, c. 1909. Trolley buses, which replaced them, operated without the rails but were still powered by overhead cables. Note the ornate gantries. (Beamish. The North of England Open Air Museum, Co. Durham)

'Big Wesley', West Hartlepool, pre-1905. This church, beautifully restored on the outside, is now a night club. (Araf Chohan)

sandstone. And last time I saw it, it was black – black as the back of the fire when you've burnt coal in it. So that's an improvement.

Yes, it says it's 'The Wesley Night Club' and it's advertising what sort of ale you can buy here! But it's a lovely building.

It's amazing what a change there is in Hartlepool. Because with my mother staying here I used to come through when I was married and it really had gone a bit seedy. It had gone down quite a lot. And I'm really quite impressed with what I've seen today. I think the centre of the town's beautiful. They've gone to a lot of trouble and good on them. It's well worth doing and I hope

lots of people come and visit the town because of it.

Jean Kendall, age 66
Hurworth, Darlington

18

CHAPTER 2

Little palaces

Early on in the project we thought it might be a good idea to take someone back to the house where they grew up, to see how it has changed. Even in the 1970s plenty of people in the region were still making do with a tin bath in the living room. It's not only the housing itself which has changed down the century. Frequently, during the course of the interviews, people would remark how we now use our homes to shut ourselves off from the rest of the world – curtains drawn and television on.

Not every home was a 'little palace'. This is the inside of a house due for slum clearance at Shildon, 1954. (Beamish. The North of England Open Air Museum, Co. Durham)

Squalor

Some people did live in squalor. Some people live in squalor in beautiful houses now. But most of the families that I knew, those houses were palaces...they were little palaces. We lived in pit villages, so we lived in coal dust. But we didn't wallow in muck. No way. No, the women saw to that.

Patricia Aspinall, age 60
Crook, Co. Durham

Joan Foster (née Leonard) outside Apple Tree Cottage, Gayles, 1950. (Joan Foster)

Gayles

Gayles is a little village beyond Richmond, between Richmond and Barnard Castle, and it's the little village where I grew up until I was thirteen years old. I've returned today, forty-seven years later, to have a look round the place and to have a look at the house where I was brought up.

The house is called Apple Tree Cottage and the apple tree is actually still in the garden. The windows – the four sash windows, two on either side – they're the same and then there is another sash window in the middle at the bottom, and that's where the front door used to be.

We're going towards what used to be the coal house but which has now obviously been modernised and is now the front entrance to the house.

Joan Foster, age 59
Norton

Wide Open

Nobody locked the doors. Our door stood open...I mean, we would go to bed and we would never lock the door. And in my own home and many others the door was opened at four o'clock in the morning, and I mean propped wide open with a weight against the front door and stood open until nine o'clock at night. And often, mum would have gone to the shop or something and the house would be empty.

Harry Peart, age 71
Darlington

Harry Peart (centre) with brothers Gilbert and Tom, in the Auxilliary Fire Service, outside his home at Cockfield, Co. Durham, in wartime. (Harry Peart)

Job Lot

I'm now in a part of the house obviously that wasn't habitable as such...this part of the house was what used to be the coal house. In this corner, you came through the coal house, the coal was all stored there and there was a closet toilet. That was the outside toilet. It was the only toilet we had. There was no running water in the house at all – not even cold water. We brought the water from taps in the street, carried it in, in buckets. And of course there wasn't any electricity.

John and Joan (crying) Leonard, 1940. Taken outside Blackburns House, Gayles. The pram was used by all the Leonard children, then loaned to another family and returned to the Leonards when the youngest, Leslie, was born in 1952. (Joan Foster)

We left in 1953 and the house was like that then. My parents rented it when they got married in 1938 from a Mr Ironson who lived in the next cottage, and the first rent that they paid was 3s 6d a week which is what? $17\frac{1}{2}$p in old money now? And the first lot of furniture they bought as a job lot at Richmond. It would be second-hand and it included crockery and whatever and it cost them £5 10s. And the reason I know all that is because my father kept a diary and I've got the diaries.

Joan Foster, age 59
Norton

Private Housing

I grew up in – which was unusual for most people in the village – I grew up in a private house. Out of the fifty-one girls in my class at school there were only three of us lived in private housing. My father tells me that when he and my mother were getting married, a house came up for sale and his father, who had lived in colliery housing all of his life, said: 'I think you should – if you can – try and buy that house.' It was £500 and they thought 'Oh, £500,' this must have been in about 1953, 'where on earth am I going to get £500?' I think they had some savings and they went to the building society, which was the Thornley Building Society, which of course doesn't exist any longer, and they were able to borrow the money.

Margaret Hedley, age 45
Durham

22

Room for Living

We're in what used to be the kitchen – what we called the kitchen, which now is the lounge, living room or whatever; and this is where we lived and ate and listened to the radio and made our mats and everything else that went on in the house. That was where the front door was so that is an extra window, and the range, the fire…now then, the oven was at that side and the boiler was at that side and it was blackleaded every Saturday morning.

Joan Foster, age 59
Norton

Bang

The whole range had to be polished and cleaned with something they called black lead. But mum had a very unusual way of cleaning all the soot and grit out from underneath. Dad was a miner and he always had a can on his belt that carried sticks of gunpowder. So mum used to take a small amount of gunpowder on a piece of paper, screw it up into a little nugget, push the nugget right underneath – the fire is out, of course – right round the back, light it with a taper and then just hold a steel sheet up in front and wait for the explosion. There was a mini 'bang', and all the soot came down and then she would just sweep it all out. I as a child was probably hiding under the bed, or something like, dreading this explosion to take place, wondering what was going to happen next. But it

Blackleading the range: Jim Howe, aged ninety, at his home in Tow Law, Co. Durham, 1957. (Beamish. The North of England Open Air Museum, Co. Durham)

happened about once a month.

Harry Peart, age 71
Darlington

Dynamite

My first real recollection was living in Broom Street in about 1925. My uncle came round and my father and uncle papered on a Sunday. They were just finishing papering and just going to put the things back and he says 'Right, get a shovel of coal and put it on the fire'. And I went out and got a shovel of coal and put it on the fire. And I'd just got back through the door

Jack Smith (standing) and his brother, Fred, practice wrestling holds on Redcar beach, 1938. (Jack Smith)

Overcrowding

So with mum and dad and six children it's a very small room, isn't it? It'd be quite crowded in here – although I don't remember it being overcrowded, but I suppose you're used to it aren't you? And as children we didn't spend a lot of time in the house to be honest, winter and summer. In the summer holidays from school we were out all day, every day. So you weren't in the house very much, all together. Obviously at meal times. Then, you knew what time you had to be home at night, ready for bed, and it was in, washed ready for bed and upstairs and that was it.

The floors were stone flags originally, and they'd be covered with what we called 'oil cloth'. It wasn't lino, it was oil cloth, with the clippy rugs that we used to make. That's how we spent winter evenings, sat round the frame with the hessian on and making clippy mats from all the old rags and that."

Joan Foster, age 59
Norton

Mats

The floor would always have proddy [clippy] mats, home-made mats, but my mother, along with most ladies in the village, got together in various…like the church hall or something, or the Salvation Army hall and they made mats. Teams of women would make mats for each other. And mother always had a mat being made somewhere. Propped up in the back kitchen would be a mat that was under construction, as

to put the coal out and there was a bang! There'd been a stick of dynamite in the coal. My father was just putting the mirror above the mantlepiece and he got the blast right in his stomach. There were no ambulances then. My uncle got a handcart – the fish shop at the corner, Beryl's fish shop – borrowed their handcart, put him on the handcart and took him up the infirmary. His shirt had a hole in it, when it was washed. The force of the explosion had pitted all his stomach. He got better.

Jack Smith, age 78
Middlesbrough

A lady makes clippy mats, Durham, in the 1930s. (Beamish. The North of England Open Air Museum, Co. Durham)

it were. It would be brought out on two trestles and mum would be sitting and probably friends who called would sit down alongside her and push the clippings through a few at a time. As children, of course, we had to cut the old clothing up into strips and sort them out into colours for mum to make what they used to call proddy mats.

Cleaning the mats and shaking the mats, mum would have to lift this heavy mat up, out through the front and wallop it against the wall, just beat it against the wall. We didn't have any carpet beaters but every day mum walloped the mats against the wall and clouds of dust came off them.

Harry Peart, age 71
Darlington

Jobs To Do

Through here was the kitchen which was long and narrow. At this end was the zinc bath where we brought the water in the buckets from outside and put it into the bath so that my mother could use the water during the day. We all had our jobs to do when we came home from school and one of the boys, that was their job to bring the water in. Another one had to chop the sticks. I had to set the table for the tea, so we all had our little jobs to do.

The zinc bath for our baths that we used to have in the sitting room hung on a nail somewhere out there. And Friday night would be bath night. I was always first in the bath because I was a girl. I always got the clean water. By the time it got round to the last boy I hate to think what the bath water would be like!

Joan Foster, age 59
Norton

smelly…I don't think we were, anyway.

Patricia Tricker, age 51
Bedale, North Yorkshire

Wanting a Bath

I suppose it was the same time, maybe, when we had the gas fire put in, but eventually the council came round and put a gas immersion heater in, which wasn't terribly efficient. It used to take ages to heat up. But I remember once wanting a bath…when I got to about fourteen or fifteen… and my dad saying 'You can't have one. You only had one last night. You can't have one.' But we weren't

Improvements

When the transition for running water and flush toilets and hot water systems came in a lot of people that I knew still carried on as they'd done before. Their daughters and sons would come and say, 'Mum, why haven't you had a proper bath?'…you know; 'Well,' they'd say, 'I didn't need it. I just washed my face.' So they had difficulty in being persuaded that these were improvements.

A back lane in Normanby, showing a water pump. The hatches in the back yard walls may be coal holes or the means by which the netty would be emptied. (Araf Chohan)

Washing day at Horden, Co. Durham, 1940s. Note the tin bath hanging on the yard wall. (Beamish. The North of England Open Air Museum, Co. Durham)

We had no flush toilet, for example. In those days we had what we called the netty, the dry midden across the yard. Sometimes it was a terrible place to go to because you had to cross the yard in the middle of winter or in pouring rain or whatever. Essentially, this was a pit where the fire ashes were tipped as well, so everything that was waste from the house went into this tip. There's a wooden seat, a hinged wooden seat on the top, so that we used to often wait until mum had gone out and emptied the fire and tipped the hot ashes out and then we'd go to the loo and do our little jobs sitting on the seat because we had this lovely warmth coming up from the hot ashes on your bum. We used to try and time it to go like that.

Harry Peart, age 71
Darlington

Laundry hanging in a back lane at New Marske. The device in the foreground is a tar pump or street disinfector. (Beamish. The North of England Open Air Museum, Co. Durham)

Poss Tub

In this corner here was where the poss tub would be…mother doing her washing.

Joan Foster, age 59
Norton

Wash Day

Washing day you know was a nightmare. They were up at five o'clock. The washing was soaked the night before and then it was possed and mangled and scrubbed and boiled and blued and rinsed and rinsed and rinsed and then mangled again…and had to be out on the line before nine o'clock. And then you had all the coal dust that would be blowing about so you brought them in and started again. It must have been an absolute nightmare. You know, when I think I go and shove mine into the machine there and turn a couple of knobs and that's them washed. And I grumble if I've got to take them to the tumble dryer. But not these women – these women were heroines!

Patricia Aspinall, age 60
Crook, Co. Durham

Illumination

Of course, you've got all the electric lights as well, whereas when we were here it would be candles, the very, very small tilly lamps with just the little base where you put paraffin in, with just a tiny little shade on it and a little, long, roundy wick in it which was sufficient for you to see where you were going. And the paraffin lamps, the bigger ones with the bowl where you put the paraffin in and the glass shade with the wick in that you turned up. And then following that, what I remember as the mantle lamp which had a pump action to it and – this is all I can remember about it – having to pump like mad. It had a mantle on it, it was like a muslin film, which you fitted to the lamp. Once you'd done the pumping you then lit it and it glowed under the glass. A great advance actually, from the little paraffin lamps.

Joan Foster, age 59
Norton

Telly for Christmas

Most of the Dales villages had power supplies by 1940, '42…somewhere about that era. But the more isolated farmsteads, a lot of them didn't get the power supplies until…certainly the mid to late '50s. I think it would be Christmas Eve when I was nineteen year old, that's when we got the first electric light and of course, the telly came for Christmas. I thought it was a great thing – one channel, black and white.

Neil Pattinson, age 57
Daddry Shield, Weardale

Electricity

We had oil lamps and candles initially, and then there was a dramatic event when the village had electricity…and we had electricity put in, very minimal number of lights, and my mother still couldn't switch the lights on. She still went around with a candle and a torch. She found it very difficult. We gradually got used to the electricity.

Harry Peart, age 71
Darlington

Flashlight

I used to sneak a flashlight to bed with me to read. Read under the covers.

Joan Foster, age 59
Norton

Calor Gas

Aye, and then to bed with a candle, no electric light. It's a wonder we didn't set ourselves on fire. Then we got Calor gas, that's right, we had Calor gas lights in the bedroom. And actually, it's unbelievable, that situation prevailed until I was nineteen year old.

Neil Pattinson, age 57
Daddry Shield, Weardale

Solid Stairs

The stairs have been turned round and they're…wooden? Yes, they're wooden stairs where originally they were stone stairs. I remember that because I fell down them. There was a stair carpet on. I've been trying to figure in my mind how you fix a stair carpet to stone stairs. There were brass stair rods

going across. That would be quite a feat getting them out, wouldn't it, breaking up stone stairs. Because they were solid.

That door there led into the next bedroom where my brothers slept. So this is the one with the fireplace. That looks like the original fireplace. That *is* the original fireplace. There would be a fender round there.

Joan Foster, age 59
Norton

Top and Tail

I think essentially the boys slept in one bedroom and the girls slept in another and we often 'topped and tailed' – you know, like one at the top of the bed and one at the bottom of the bed. Mum and dad always seemed to sleep downstairs. They had a sort of what we would now call a put-you-up settee or something similar to that, and basically that's how the family was split up.

Harry Peart, age 71
Darlington

Sleepwalk

There would be four of my brothers would sleep in here because Leslie was born in 1952 and he slept downstairs with my parents. So four of my brothers would sleep in here. There was two double beds…I think John and Dennis slept together and Jim and Frank slept together. So there was a bed down that side and a bed down that side and there was a wardrobe over on that wall there. Because my twin brother,

The Leonard children of Apple Tree Cottage, Gayles, 1953. From left to right: John and Joan (twins; Joan holding Leslie), Dennis, James, with Frank at the front. (Joan Foster)

John, he used to sleepwalk. And he climbed up the wardrobe one night and brought it over on himself. I think he must have imagined he was climbing a wall and he brought the wardrobe over onto himself.

Joan Foster, age 59
Norton

Own Bedroom

Nearly all of my friends who had sisters shared a bedroom and I had a bedroom to myself and I always felt pretty special because of that. I never wanted to share it with anyone either. I never wanted brothers and sisters. I remember that, particularly when I was in the fifth year in the girls' school in Wheatley Hill, it was a very small number in the class – I think there were only ten of us, and if it ever came to the crunch where we had to go to someone's house it was usually mine and it was often in my bedroom because it was quite a big room. It had two beds in it, and it was nicely done out by the late '60s.

My father built fitted wardrobes which were up and coming, over an old fireplace in the room. That was taken out, but the chimney breast was still there and we'd seen these fitted wardrobes where you built over the chimney breast into the alcove to make it look a flush wall. And these wardrobes were special. They were really, really good and I can remember that I could choose the bedding and the curtains, and everything was bright orange because orange was the colour. It must have looked horrendous but at the time I was so proud of this bedroom. Everything was new in it, you know, the wardrobes were new and the carpet; and there was a new window put in there, a big new window, and a bedside table with an orange top and these – horrible now – orange bedspreads! But I suppose at the time they were really modern. Orange was the colour in the '60s and I was so proud of this bedroom.

Margaret Hedley, age 45
Durham

My Bedroom

We're in what used to be my bedroom now and there was another cupboard in the corner where my father kept books and things. My bed was along here and there was a washstand with the bowl and the jug on. A couple of chairs, possibly, that's all I remember. I think there was a chest of drawers and then from my bedroom …the door…you see this door wouldn't be here. It's all been altered, this.

Joan Foster, age 59
Norton

Sharing

Looking back at it, I don't think I ever have had my own room. I don't think I have, no. We were still sharing a bedroom, my brother and me – two brothers actually, by then. And then I got married and didn't get any peace – I had the bedroom to share with the wife, you see!

Neil Pattinson, age 57
Daddry Shield, Weardale

Apple Tree

It's amazing, looking out and all the birds…I'm pleased to see that apple tree is still there. I don't know why. There were two things I wanted to see if they were still there. The apple tree – isn't it odd? And the stone stairs. But it's been fascinating looking round it, actually, it really has. It brings back lots and lots of happy memories.

Joan Foster, age 59
Norton

CHAPTER 3

A cosmopolitan collective

Almost everyone on Teesside, it seems, is an immigrant – perhaps their ancestors were Vikings; more likely they moved into the area from surrounding villages to take advantage of the booming industrial employment of the late nineteenth century. The twentieth century has seen a new wave of immigration from overseas. We asked people how they came to be here and what being a Teessider means to them.

THE TEES

MIDDLESBROUGH – THE PRINCIPAL CENTRE OF IRON AND STEEL INDUSTRY – STOCKTON AND SOUTH BANK FOR SHIPBUILDING ADJACENT HOLIDAY RESORTS – REDCAR AND SALTBURN

LONDON AND NORTH EASTERN RAILWAY

LNER poster entitled 'Famous Rivers of Commerce – The Tees', 1930s. The original painting was by Frank Mason. (Beamish. The North of England Open Air Museum, Co. Durham)

Heugher

I was born in Old Hartlepool. I was born in Winston Street which is no longer there. It was under Throston Bridge which is no longer there. But if you were born on the yon side of Throston Bridge then you were known as a 'Heugher', so I'm a Heugher. If you were born at West Hartlepool you were a 'Poolie'. But I'm a Heugher and very proud of it.

Margo Coser, age 68
Hartlepool

Villages

It must take a thousand years for a town to gain an identity but they were just all little villages, you know; when my dad was a lad it was Eston, Normanby, Redcar, Marske, Ormsby; they all had their own little village identity and they were all in Yorkshire.

Vin Garbutt, age 52
Loftus

British

I think I became aware as a nine year old who I was. I have always thought of myself first and foremost…as a youngster I would have said English but as you grow up you realise there are definitions. So I always say British now, because unless you have both parents born in England you are not English. It doesn't matter what colour, nationality, whatever religion they are; you can class yourself as English if your parents are born here. So my parents weren't born here. We were therefore British, and

Eston seen from Eston Banks, *c.* 1902. The ironstone mine is prominent. The picture illustrates how rural these areas were at this time. (Araf Chohan)

The fitting-out basin at Furness' Shipyard, Haverton Hill, 1951. (Bert Ward)

I've always first of all thought of myself as British. Secondly has been my religion, and then thirdly my cultural background as I grew older and became aware and could define the very many differences and nuances of Asian life. Just to be a Punjabi you could be a Sikh, a Moslem or a Hindu. To anybody else it's like you looking at Northern Ireland and saying 'Um, are you a Catholic or a Protestant?' or whatever. You wouldn't tell the difference because the voice, the culture, the dress and everything would be the same.

Bari Chohan, age 49
Sedgefield

Normanby

My dad is from Normanby. The Garbutts are from Normanby. His parents came to work in Teesside from out in Yorkshire – Thirsk area. Normanby was traditionally Anglo-Saxon Protestant, and South Bank – a lot of the Irish people were down there, you see, so it was a very Catholic area. They were only two miles apart – in fact, they're all joined up at the minute – but South Bank in those days was…there was a lot of Irish people there, or second-generation Irish. And never the twain…my mam used to say there was always fights on the trunk

35

road near where the Eston baths are now, years and years ago when she was a young lass so we're on about 1920 or something. Anyway, she met our dad, English Protestant; she was an Irish Catholic. They got married and never had any trouble.

Vin Garbutt, age 52
Loftus

Italy

My grandfather settled in Middlesbrough – had a look round and managed to rent a place in Middlesbrough. He went back to Italy. Don't ask me how he acquired this wife

Nafees Chohan in 1953, four years after her arrival in England. (Araf Chohan)

but he came back married and decided that there wasn't enough business for two, so he went his way and he went to Stockton and the other brother stayed in Middlesbrough. He found a nice place on the corner of Yarm Lane. They made ice cream there and had a café, ice cream parlour, and then he opened places all over the place."

George Pacitto, age 58
Redcar

To England

I married, I stay one night at his house and my auntie with me, then we come back. Then he came 1948 in the January, come back. And he ask my mother 'Will she come into the station?' And I was just a kid, you know, not mean anything. Then he said in the station 'Are you understand you're old enough – you're nearly fifteen and I want to take you in England.' I say, 'I don't want to go in England. I don't leave my mum.' And that's all I said to him. Anyhow, he come back, he sent me ticket. Then he wrote a letter to my oldest cousin. He's working in High Court in Lahore. He's a secretary. Then he come in our village where we lived, he say, 'Auntie, look, she have to go in England.' I was screaming, I was crying, I didn't want to leave my own home. I don't know him. Then my cousin say, 'Listen, Nafees, you're married. You're sixteen. You're lady.' I say, 'I'm not damn lady, hinny, I don't know what this mean. I don't want him, I don't like him.' He say, 'You have to go.'

Nafees Chohan, age 68
Middlesbrough

Punjab

There were no women, other than my mother, in the early '50s. There was one Sikh family from the early '50s, and eventually one Indian family. When I say family, with a woman and children. Luckily, those three families were ethnically the same. We were from an area of India called Punjab, but we were three different religions and although in the ensuing years it's been difficult because of the problems on the sub-continent it engendered a very close warmth between all the communities here on Teesside because the early people went to each other's weddings and they were culturally the same. They spoke the same language although they were religiously different.

Bari Chohan, age 49
Sedgefield

Ghulam Chohan, father of Bari, in 1938. He arrived in England as a teenager in the mid-1930s. (Araf Chohan)

Like a Daughter

In '52, a Sikh family come in North Ormsby. After thirteen days the fellow died. And Mr Chohan said, 'Come on, you know, there's some more Asian family come. You should be pleased.' I said, 'Who?' He said, 'The fellow, he was Middlesbrough and he's bringing a family and he's died thirteen day after his family come.' My boy is, I think, three weeks old. I say, 'I want to go. I'm dying to go and see them.' Well, anyhow, after a couple of days, when the weekend come, he's not working, he took me.

We went about half an hour, say one hour…we come home. After six month, this older lady come to my house with her son. She says, 'Same time I see you, I think you're my daughter. I've got no daughter.' I say 'Listen. You are Sikh. We are Moslem. I can't agree with you. Coming into your house, you come in my house yes, friend. But don't call me daughter.' Anyhow, Mr Chohan come. He say, 'Ah, howay, don't break that lady's heart.' Anyhow, she did treat me like a daughter.

Nafees Chohan, age 68
Middlesbrough

Blending In

Again, going back thirty odd years, Charles Amier used to have a Neapolitan night for the Italian communities…and it was quite full, it could fill a ballroom, so yeah, there was plenty of them about. But I thought, well, much as I like quite a lot of them, it wasn't really my scene because I was English through and through. Some of them were very good friends of mine but in general we keep our own council, we stick to our own business and we're not attached to anybody else's. I think that's how it should be. You should sort of blend into your surroundings, as it were. Well, I think so.

George Pacitto, age 58
Redcar

No Different

Overall, I tend to think that we are very fortunate in that, having been the only Asian family brought up in Middlesbrough and Teesside for many years, all the way through our infant, junior, secondary and senior school, it was certainly not evident ourselves of any major racial problems. I certainly never recall any problems like this throughout my life. You're always going to have some reference, but I find that it was just as prevalent for somebody if he's ginger or Irish or a handicapped person…they were no more likely to say 'golliwog' rather than anything else because there was no differential, there was no yardstick. So all the way through our schooling we were the same as anybody else. The fact that we were a

Redcar High Street, prior to the age of the motor car. (Beamish. The North of England Open Air Museum, Co. Durham)

St John's School, Middlesbrough in 1962. Bari Chohan is on the back row, fourth from left. There were few children from Asian families in Middlesbrough at that time. (Araf Chohan)

bit darker, but we were totally British and English and spoke with the same language and local inflection in our voices. Therefore there was nothing for us to be different.

Bari Chohan, age 49
Sedgefield

Pharaoh

I had an allotment here in Loftus and there was one young black lad living in Loftus at the time. 'Pharaoh', they called him. And the lad on the allotment next to me saw Pharaoh walking past. And he's ginger-headed, this lad on the next allotment. And he said, 'Look at that.' I said, 'What?' He said, 'Blacks, taking over the country.' And I said, 'Who, Pharaoh?' He said, 'Yes, they're all over the place.' I said,

'Hey, he's only ten, you know, and he's hardly likely to think of taking over the country yet.' 'Oh,' he says, 'it's not just him. I've been to Birmingham,' he says, 'they've taken over in Birmingham.' I said, 'Well, I go to Bradford a lot and I remember reading once that the crime rate was halved with the influx of Asians there,' I said, 'so there was a point when I thought there were too many whites in Bradford for its own good.'

So anyway, this ginger-haired lad's listening to me and I said, 'Your ancestors must have had a bit of bother when they arrived in England.' He says, 'Oh, my ancestors are all English.' I said, 'Bloomin' heck, you've got a shock of ginger hair there,' I says, 'They were probably Celts!' I says, 'and when the Celts got here they probably got loads of gyp off the local Brits,' I says, 'Because even today Brits can be pretty hard on people.'

He's leaning on his spade and I said 'What school does your kids go to?' He said, 'Hummersea.' Hummersea School at Loftus. 'Oh,' I said, 'Well, when the Vikings first settled here,' I said, 'your ancestors have probably got a bit of Celt, and a bit of Norwegian or Danish.' 'Oh,' he says, 'There's no Danish or Norwegian in my family!' 'Oh,' I said, 'Hummer's "humma". Humma is Scandinavian for lobster.' I said, 'There's still lobster pots down the road there, because the Vikings used to put their pots out here. And all these local names…'

And he even used an expression, he said he was 'fit as a lop'. And of course, a lop is a flea in Scandinavia. He didn't know what a lop was – in fact I didn't at that time until I looked it up, because I've always said, 'fit as a lop'. Fit as a flea, you see. And what else did he say? 'Liggin'. He was on about people not working. He said, 'Oh, they come over here', he says, 'and they're liggin' all day.' I says, 'What do you mean, "liggin"?' He says, 'They're lying down, they won't get up, won't do nowt.'

And of course, that's the German verb, isn't it, 'liegen', for laying down. So anyway, I was chucking all these foreign bits that he obviously had. And it did the trick actually. It was like a compact lesson in genealogy because he just sort of went quiet and looked pensive. I went back to digging. Then he came over to me a bit later. He said, 'I haven't travelled as much as you, you know.'

To go to London and south of, is like going abroad for me. I have to accept that it is a different culture. Reading in Berkshire is my favourite hate-place. I remember standing in a bus queue and there was a poor chap with a walking stick, he couldn't get on the bus. And the whole queue behind him were looking…nobody would help him, they all looked really awkward. Embarrassed. They're saying, 'What's this fellow doing to us?' you know. And I was at the back of the queue. I couldn't believe it. I walked to the front, helped him on the bus – I'm no great Samaritan, I was just doing what would be average and normal on Teesside – but nobody in that queue was interested in helping this handicapped chap onto the bus. I got him on and then went back to the back of the queue. And not without tutting, by the way, on the way back to my place.

Vin Garbutt, age 52
Loftus

Lads Together

But it was amazing how many lads were down there from the 'Borough, how many lads were down there from Sunderland. I bumped into very few Geordies but mostly Sunderland lads and 'Borough lads were down there. And we had quite a good little friendship developing, you know. We used to go drinking…obviously there'd be good banter there. We used to sit in the pub at a weekend and look at the Ceefax – because obviously they were only interested in Southern teams, a lot of the lads, but we would get the Ceefax off them and see the scores, and you know, a bit of banter there. But at the end of the day, we were down there working as one really, and I think in

Roseberry Topping from Newton under Roseberry. (Beamish. The North of England Open Air Museum, Co. Durham)

some respects…you come to rely on each other because you become each other's family. You know, watching out for each other, helping each other. Which is nice in many respects.

Paul Evans, age 31
Middlesbrough

5,000 Miles

Perth, in Australia, I do a regular concert and I fly by night. Freemantle, actually. And a couple of days before the concert, I arrived early to get rid of my jetlag; I was sat outside this café having a cup of cappuccino, and there was a building site just up the road and these two fellows were walking across the road, with hard hats on, overalls. And one of them shouted, 'Hey, Vinny!' he says, 'How yer doing?' I says, 'Hey, all right Alan, how you getting on?' He says, 'By, brilliant mate. How's yer dad?' I says, 'Ah, smashing.' He says, 'Is he still going to the club?' I said, 'No, he doesn't get about as much as he used to.' He said, 'Hey, love to stop and talk to you but I have to get to work.'

Now, this was…how many? 5,000 miles away from home and it was as though I was in Eston Square. He just carried on with his business after passing the time of day with me. Brilliant!

Vin Garbutt, age 52
Loftus

41

The Transporter Bridge, Middlesbrough, 1966, photographed by Frank Atkinson. This is a view from the north side. (Beamish. The North of England Open Air Museum, Co. Durham)

Middlesbrough

So I've been here forty-nine year in this road. It's all changed, Middlesbrough. Sometime just thinking about it, it's a dream. Middlesbrough very, very small, used to be. And is all growing now, this way. And now, is everywhere you go, houses. And a big shopping centre...used to be no shopping centre in here, nothing. Middlesbrough, it was nothing.

Nafees Chohan, age 68
Middlesbrough

CHAPTER 4

Going between houses

The way of life in the North Pennine Dales has remained largely unchanged for centuries. However, with old industries like lead mining gone and with hill farming facing serious problems, more and more young people are leaving the Dales to seek a future elsewhere. They are replaced by commuters or people looking for a peaceful place for retirement. The Dales have to come to terms with a new sense of who belongs.

Daddry Shield, Weardale, c. 1955. The post office has closed and the telephone box has been replaced by one of modern design on the opposite side of the road. Otherwise, little has changed since this picture was taken. (Neil Pattinson)

Dales People

We're all Dales people…there's something about the Dales – it doesn't matter, Wensleydale, Swaledale, wherever you go – Allendale – you've all got something very much in common. It's just a way of life. It's an established way of life and it's dying out, but we were all part of that set-up.

Ray Dent, age 80
Daddry Shield, Weardale

Decline

I think it changed the most rapidly in the latter part of the 1970s. It was the latter part of the 1970s when unemployment really began to take hold in the Upper Dale. Prior to that we'd had high levels of employment. There was virtually nobody unemployed. There were mines. Quarries, cement works. There were also some projects such as the Kielder aqueduct, the construction of that, the construction of the cement works, the construction of a new fluorspar development at Blackdene Mine. So within each eight-year period there was some new civil engineering project that ran alongside the local employment. But sadly we came to the latter end of the 1970s, there was no more large-scale developments. The traditional industries began a very rapid decline, and at that stage, you know, many of the young people left this village and other villages to seek employment elsewhere and it was at that moment in time that it became the biggest change

that I've certainly seen in the way of life of the Dale.

Neil Pattinson, age 57
Daddry Shield, Weardale

Helping Out

When I came to Wearhead, neighbours were very friendly. You chatted. A lot of that sort of thing, which I hadn't done in Consett – well, not with neighbours. If you had an accident or anything, people used to come and clean your house out, or something like that, and help out, in the village. When I first came to Wearhead that did exist, definitely, for a lot of years. And still does to some extent. People help each other out – but they help each other out in all kinds of places, not just in Weardale, don't they? But there is a bit of that sort of thing still exists. There seemed to be a lot of…going between houses. Do you know what that is?

Margery Lonsdale, age 59
Wearhead, Weardale

There When Needed

The old-fashioned way of 'if you were in trouble, I was in trouble, boy'. In fact, my wife died suddenly and the neighbours that come in…people come, they were there. They were there when you needed them. And some of my old friends. I was left at a loose end. My family of course was there, but there's about four or five houses, probably six or seven, after that happened, I was fed up with myself, I could go and walk in the

Mystery surrounds this splendid portrait. Although it is understood to have been taken in Daddry Shield, nobody seems to know who these two people are. (Neil Pattinson)

door and spend two hours there. You know, that's the sort of thing – unmentioned, nothing mentioned – it was just an unseen thing.

Ray Dent, age 80
Daddry Shield, Weardale

Neighbourly

I lived in a cottage, we bought a little cottage and it was semi-detached. The neighbour next door, from day one, looked after the house. And if I went out, we didn't lock the door. She used to come in and we had a coal fire and she'd build the fire up and bring the washing in. And that was the way it operated.

Margery Lonsdale, age 59
Wearhead, Weardale

After Chapel

The church and the chapel was the focus of all the social life. It was a social night out, the Sunday night at the chapel. I mean, more often than not, in them days, you went to chapel and either somebody come back for supper or you went to somebody else's house for supper. The funny thing about it in those days, nearly every house, somebody could play some instrument. Fiddle, an old organ, mouth organ and after the chapel you'd probably go to somebody's house and have supper, then the music would start. Mostly hymns, mind, and you'd have half an hour singing hymns before you came home.

Ray Dent, age 80
Daddry Shield, Weardale

Dancing

I was a member of the local dramatic society in the 1950s for twelve years. We gave a production in the local town hall in St John's Chapel every March. And we had a local old-time dance club in every village. Cowshill had an old-time dance club, St John's Chapel, Westgate, Stanhope, Frosterley, Wolsingham, Witton le Wear all had an old-time dance club. And we had a dance at Cowshill every fortnight, every alternate Monday. We visited other village dances too and then there was the weekend dances in the local town hall at St John's Chapel.

Arnold Lonsdale, age 68
Wearhead, Weardale

Clipping

It made a big difference when we got clipping machines for shearing the sheep. Aye. When it was done by hand it was a social occasion because you put a clipping day on and all your neighbours from other sheep farms come round. It was a meeting. There wasn't a machine going, it was hand clipping. Conversation never lagged. It went on and on and on.

Ray Dent, age 80
Daddry Shield, Weardale

Lonely Life

The life of a Dales farmer has become a much more lonely life. When farms were small, whatever job he was

Neil Pattinson (left) with brother Michael, and Audrey Redman at Pinfold Farm, Daddry Shield, Weardale, c. 1947. (Neil Pattinson)

doing his neighbour in the next field was doing a similar job. There was always time to chat. But now it's left as a one-man band, rushing and tearing everywhere, nobody to chat to. And then the outcome of that, they tell us that the suicide rate amongst the farming community is the highest of anything in the UK.

Neil Pattinson, age 57
Daddry Shield, Weardale

Sixth Generation

I'm the sixth generation to farm in Upper Weardale, and I hope my son will continue to farm afterwards, after I'm gone.

My ancestors lived where the reservoir is now, in the old farm house called Dyke Head. Fortunately this farm became vacant in 1932 and my father was fortunate to get the tenancy. Just a matter of 200 yards away. It was adjoining the land at Dyke Head and they came to Pryhill in 1932, when I was two year old. So I spent the first two years of my life where the reservoir is now!

My grandparents found it a great upheaval, put it that way. They were in their seventies then. My grandfather died in 1936 and they never fully recovered. Even though they were moving such a short distance, the work of the reservoir starting, seeing farm houses covered with water. Most of the farm houses were demolished and the stone was crushed up and put into the reservoir embankment. All this activity – they had narrow-gauge railways criss-crossing all over; they had a quarry up on the hillside and they were bringing stone out of the quarry and it was so

47

foreign to them. You see, a lot of the land was submerged. They still retained the sheep right up on the hill, but the farmhouse and all the surrounding land was submerged. They came here and grandfather and grandmother only survived for a few years afterwards.

Arnold Lonsdale, age 68
Wearhead, Weardale

Broad Teesdale

In the first place, we were farming in Teesdale and things were so bad. In those days there was no tenancy agreement. A tenant could be put off a farm without any hassle or anything like that. It just so happened that the landlord's farm across there, his son-in-law wanted it. So we had to get out. Things were bad and this job came up as manager at the farm in Weardale and father applied for it. He was the hundred and twenty-first applicant when he put his name forward and he got the job. That was in 1929.

We came over here and I had the Mickey taken out of me, because I was broad Teesdale, when we come to Westgate school. You're coming to a different language – well, it was the same language, but different tone and everything – different ways of expressing yourself. And it took me a bit before you sort of fell into it.

Ray Dent, age 80
Daddry Shield, Weardale

Presents

I came to live in Weardale in 1965 from Consett. When I came to live in Weardale, when I married Arnold, I was accepted, because I'd married a local lad. And the thing that amazed me more than anything when I came to live in the village, was after we came back from our honeymoon, and we went round with the milk on the morning after we were back, we were given about twenty presents or thirty presents. It was absolutely amazing. The milk customers came to the door with all these wedding presents wrapped up. And that was a tradition in Weardale, and still is to some extent. People do give wedding presents who they're not going to the wedding. Little presents, you know, nice little things. And I thought, 'What a wonderful thing!' Of course, obviously, it was Arnold they were giving the presents to, but me – I was on cloud nine, I didn't realise at the time that it was obviously, 'Well, he's been a very good milkman. We'll have to give Arnold a present, he's getting married.' But I didn't think that then, I thought 'How very kind they are to me!'

Margery Lonsdale, age 59
Wearhead, Weardale

Loggerheads

There was always aggro in the Dales, I mean, even in this dale, there was always that village community that was at loggerheads with the next village community. I mean, and some of that's still lingering today. Not in any bad form, but it keeps getting mentioned,

'Oh, he belongs there,' and that sort of thing, you know.

They tell me at one time – same thing happened in Teesdale mind, not in my time – but if a lad was courting a girl from another village he got stoned out! I mean, it's been conditioned into them. It's dying out now because the people that I knew that were guilty of that, they're probably dead or they're very old now. But there's been that little bit of…well, you cannot call it aggro…just, I don't know…a feeling.

Ray Dent, age 80
Daddry Shield, Weardale

Sunday Mornings

When we first came to the Dale, we came to live in Frosterley. The vicarage at Frosterley had been sold against the will of the people and the community, but because I think it was recognised Frosterley was unlikely ever again to have a resident vicar. And the diocese bought, as a vicarage for Frosterley, a house on a new estate in Frosterley. The first Sunday morning we were here we had no responsibilities in any of the churches and we were having a Sunday at home together. I looked out of the window and discovered that we really were on a new, modern estate where what most people did on a Sunday morning was wash the car and put the lawn sprinkler on. And I thought, 'Heck! We don't own a lawn sprinkler, and I've never washed the car on a Sunday morning.' In fact, if it gets washed twice a year it's really very lucky. 'How on earth are we going to cope on this estate?'

In the end in fact we made friends quite readily with out neighbours, who, I think, kind of accepted those eccentric clergy who didn't have lawn sprinklers

Hard winters in Weardale. The road to the school at St John's Chapel, 1947. (Neil Pattinson)

and seemed to go around in the most ramshackle vehicles possible. But it was a very odd experience. This was suburbia transported into the village community, and I think that's very difficult and it takes a long time for those communities to kind of shake down and get to know each other.

Revd Penny Jones, age 40
Stanhope, Weardale

Incomers

Even today, occasionally, very occasionally, you'll get a group of people together and they'll start to talk about 'incomers' in my presence and I have to point out to them that I'm an incomer. They say, 'Ah we don't think of you as one of them!'

But I don't want to make too much of it because I feel as if it's tret with humour in quite a lot of ways. And there is a little bit of chat about incomers but it is tinged with humour – not cynicism but humour, really, a little bit of that about it.

Margery Lonsdale, age 59
Wearhead, Weardale

Changing Attitudes

Since the war, attitudes have changed so much. But up 'til, probably 1920s, life and beliefs hadn't changed for probably two hundred years. And then all of a sudden everything's been thrown at us. And the change in this last fifty year...I wouldn't like to visualise what the changes'll be in the next fifty years, compared to what I've seen in my time.

Ray Dent, age 80
Daddry Shield, Weardale

Shovelling snow in St John's Chapel, 1947. (Neil Pattinson)

50

CHAPTER 5

The matrimonial market

The regret I heard expressed most often during the course of the interviews was the decline in marriage and the stable family. Attitudes have changed and many younger people look on marriage as an option to consider alongside careers, travel and so on. Human jealousies, emotions and frailties have not altered so much over time.

Janet Jackman aged twenty-one, in 1942. She sent this photograph to her husband-to-be, Bob, who was captured at Dunkirk. He carried it with him throughout his captivity, including a forced march through the Bavarian Alps. They married on his return in 1945. (Janet Jackman)

George Robinson with bride Maureen, Ryhope, Sunderland, 1967. (George Robinson, with permission of Northeast Press Ltd, *Sunderland Echo*)

Had to Marry

I was nineteen when I first got married and I was pregnant. And my husband, who was about ten year older than me, said 'You can't possibly be pregnant because I've had an accident and I can't have children.' And he really meant that. My mother took me to the doctor's and the doctor said, 'Are you courting, love?'

I said, 'Oh, yes.' He said, 'Well, you're pregnant.'

So my mother…straight up there, he had to marry me. I didn't want to get married. I remember I was stood at the railway station in Middlesbrough – I'd been to sign off the dole. I needn't have done but in my innocence I thought, because I was getting married I had to sign off the dole. There was a lady there with a kiddie and a pushchair. And I'm stood there and I said to her, 'I'm getting married today.' And I always remember what she said: 'Well you don't look very happy about it, honey!'

Margaret Greaves, age 86
Thornaby

Young Enough

I got married when I was twenty and we had our children when I was young – twenty-one when our Simon came along – but by the time he was eighteen I was thirty-nine year old. I wasn't forty. And we could go into the pub and I was still young enough to be able to stand alongside him in the pub and say 'It's your turn, pal!'

George Robinson, age 52
Redcar

Jealousy

He was a businessman, and he was a clever lad. It was a shame he drank a lot. And he was very, very jealous. When I was younger I used to be bonny and I used to have long black hair and voluptuous, you know, but you don't realise how good you are when you're younger, you know – you could have done better. But my mother said 'You'll have to marry her,' so we got married and he said to me, 'You'll only live with me five year, and in about five year we'll be finished.

And he used to knock me about because he was very, very jealous.

Margaret Greaves, age 86
Thornaby

Black and Blue

Ooh there was a lot of violence about. Women stayed with their husbands. I mean, I know – I worked on the district. And I couldn't even understand it then because I'd never come up against it. I mean, my own family, there was nothing like that. They were black and blue where they'd been kicked about, and black-eyed…but their husbands were just drunkards and they stayed with them because they had other children. Where else could they go? And I'd tell them, 'I wouldn't live with him two minutes. I'd kill him!', you know, but – no, they accepted it.

Catherine Bregazzi, age 86
Middlesbrough

Final Straw

He hit me on the nose and ooh, the blood used to fly and I had black eyes. I always went for the policeman. There was always a policeman about. One of the policemen said to me, 'Why don't you hit him back, honey, you're as big as him?'

And I said to him, 'Eeh, no, I might hurt him.'

But the final straw came. We were in the kitchen and we were arguing about something. My little daughter was there, she was only tiny. He thought the world of her, of course…so we were arguing and she was crying and he said, 'Go to your mother,' and he pushed her. That was it. He was on the floor in no time and he was bleeding. I'd picked up a vase – there was flowers in the vase – I'd taken them out all suddenly and bashed him. And he was down. She said, 'Eh, mother, he's bloodin', he's bloodin'!' I said 'Never mind!' and I dragged him away.

And he summoned me for it! We went to the court – oh, it wouldn't happen today – I said 'Well, I was provoked!' And the clerk said, 'No provocation', fined me five shilling. He was there as well, he paid the five shilling and he said, 'Come on home with me!' Well, you know what I told him, in no uncertain words!…and so – I did go home – eventually.

He said, 'Well, I'll never divorce you.' In those times there was no legal aid. So after fourteen years, legal aid come along and I thought, 'What shall I have for nothing? Oh, I'll have a divorce.' And I did! I went to Leeds assizes and I always remember what the judge said. He said, 'This marriage should never have taken place.' That was in '50. In '52 I was married again.

A lot of people were separated. They didn't get divorced, they were separated. I used to rub out with a chap all the time that I was separated. And of course, he was married. And he'd been to India since he was sixteen. But in 1939 when they needed the men he was invalided out as 'unfit for any other military service'. He was a big, strapping young man, he was lovely. So as soon as I got my divorce, I married him. And we had a wonderful married life, we were wonderful together.

Margaret Greaves, age 86
Thornaby

Tough Nuts

Well, you and your generation have been brought up on the 'Andy Capp' cartoons, but I think in all honesty that the Andy Capp was partly created by the women themselves so that the men believed that they were gaffers. But I've known some what were so-called pretty tough nuts amongst the men and maybe they had a fairly long lead, but I think most of them knew how long the lead was and never went beyond the end of it!

The women used to know how to handle the men and they did. The bloke would be cracking up at work how he was gaffer and how he cracked the whip and that, but he didn't dare say that he was only on a leash of so long, you know.

Walter Nunn, age 78
Shildon

Support

People have different interests. My grandmother was particularly interested in the family. Her family. My mother and her brother, and her grandchildren and so on. She liked things like that. She was a keen church-goer, she was a member of the Women's Institute and Guild and so on, and she had her own circle of friends and she went to her meetings and this, that and the other…and he had his. And I think they had a happy marriage. They weren't in one another's pockets, but they supported each other. She supported him in the way that she could, by doing the traditional things for him, ironing his shirts and all this, and he did what he considered to be his duty, he earned the money and paid the bills. They were a very happy couple. I never once heard them utter a cross word to each other.

Colin Berwick, age 66
Brotton

So Happy Together

We'd been married seven years then, seven and a half years. And we were reading. And I said to him,

Colin Berwick's grandfather, Richard Harrison, (back row, far left), with the North Skelton Silver Band, in 1920s. (Colin Berwick)

Colin Berwick's grandmother, Rose Harrison, in fancy dress in the 1920s. Rule Britannia! (Colin Berwick)

'Oh, put that down,' I said, 'I'm sick of reading.'

He said 'Yes, so am I.' And he put it down and died.

I was devastated. I wanted to gas myself. I knew…when these people go out…he'll want me with him, because we were always together. 'He'll want me with him.' I wouldn't have gone with him, would I, because according to the Lord, if you commit suicide you're not accepted into the Kingdom of Heaven.

However, nobody could talk to me. I cried and I cried. We were so happy together. After three weeks I went back to the buses, because I had a house on mortgage. And I used to go to work and the driver would turn round and I'd be crying. And they didn't know what to say to me, I was making them miserable when I went in the canteen. So I made up my mind that I wasn't going to cry at work any more. I would wait until I got home and I would go to bed and I'd have a good cry.

Margaret Greaves, age 86
Thornaby

Always Two

I'm very conscious as a widower how it is to be without your partner, but it's in the little things as well as the big things. I didn't realise how much we had talked about and how much we had shared. Even silly things, small things that might be bothering me or either of us – or little details, 'What do you think about this,' or, 'What are we going to do about that?' There are always two of you taking the decisions or making the decisions and that, I think, I found probably the hardest thing to make the adjustment in the early days. I used to try and think about what she might have said – I might not have agreed with it and I could then have a fictional argument with her and whether I did it or not would be another matter. I suppose it's another way of managing it.

John Starr, age 52
Middleton St George

Womaniser

I met a bus driver. He belonged Darlington and I belonged Middlesbrough. But we used to meet in Ferryhill in the canteen. We got talking and he was talking about the farm that his father was a hand on. And I'd worked on a farm. So we talked about the same things, you see; 'Oh do you remember so and so…'

So therefore he would say to me, 'We'll have a date.' I was a widow then, so he come to my house, you see. And I should have got the light, because he was married but they were parted and he lived in a little attic somewhere in Darlington. I went out with him, and after five year I married him.

So he took me to this farmhouse and it was derelict. And the rent wasn't much. So I sold my house and we bought pigs and all sorts. Mind you, saying that, he was very hard-working. And he was up first thing in the morning feeding those pigs and one thing and another. But we were both working on the buses, so he'd come up a bit you see, hadn't he? And when he used to go in the local at High Coniscliffe, the Spotted Dog, people used to think – especially the women –

Iris Dixon's wedding, 1944. It was a whirlwind wartime romance. (Iris Dixon)

that he was a farmer, you know. And he didn't make them any the wiser. I mean, the lads would say, 'What have you got in now, Ray?' He'd say, 'Oh, I've got so many pigs.' so the women would be cocking their eyes up, you know. He was a proper womaniser. But he was a nice fellow. But I wouldn't put up with that. I didn't have to put up with that. But his friend, who went about with him, his wife committed suicide over it with him being a womaniser. So she must have loved him, mustn't she?

Margaret Greaves, age 86
Thornaby

Hung

I worked with a fellow a number of years ago – we were on night shift.

Night shift used to start at nine o'clock on a night. You used to get your pay at the time office before you went up. You used to put your card in. And this particular time – he come from West Auckland, somewhere down that area – he come without his card, went back home for it. He didn't come to work. Two days later they found him swinging by the bloody neck on a tree. He'd hung himself. For why? Then it eventually came out. His missus had been boying about. That's what he'd done.

John Collinson, age 75
Shildon

Better at Home

I'm a very sexy woman. I don't demand it but I never, ever had a headache,

58

never. Which brings me back to Ray, who philandered. He said to me one day, I'll always remember it, 'I don't know why I bother. I've got better at home.'

And he never ever bothered any more – oh well, he did. And she was the awfullest looking woman. And he had met them in this pub. This woman was being housemaid to this older woman. It was this older woman – maybe about as old as I am now, but they were very well off. And they had dogs. Dogs get you talking. So he would run them home. So this girl cottoned on to him.

Even after I divorced him I used to go and see him. I said to him one day, 'What do you see in her, Ray?' He said, 'Well, Meg, she does my washing.'

Margaret Greaves, age 86
Thornaby

Marriage

We're only going back twenty-eight years but for me it would have been unheard of to live with him before we got married. You know, it was marriage and that was it – we got married. It's a big change isn't it?

Caroline McGough, age 48
Middlesbrough

Married Life

I love married life. I like somebody to come home to. And when I met Joe, the schoolmaster, I didn't think there were men like him. He was so honest. Mind you, he had an eye for a pretty girl. Most men have. But he thought there was nobody like me. And I used to say, 'Sit there and I'll go and clean the

John Collinson (front), doing maintenance work on the weighbridge, Shildon Shops, 1947. (John Collinson)

Richard and Liza Barrigan, great-grandparents of Pat Aspinall, on the marriage of their daughter Agnes to Ted Howarth, Esh Winning, 1930. (Pat Aspinall)

oven.' 'Oh, well I usually do that.' 'Well, you're not doing it. I'll clean the oven!'

And then he had the loveliest garden and I'd go, 'I'm going to dead-head the roses.' 'Oh, well I usually do that!' 'Well, I'm going to do it.' He had a big dishwasher, and there was only two of us. I said, 'You can get rid of that. I'm the dishwasher here!'

Margaret Greaves, age 86
Thornaby

Role Reversal

At the moment, housework comes last. My job comes first. But I'm very lucky in an unlucky way. It's that my husband was a bricklayer up 'til '94 and got really bad angina so he couldn't go back to brick laying. When he came out of work with angina he was very angry – proud man, always been physical, worked in brick laying with all the blokes – proper man's man in a way, liked his Gazette and his football and a couple of pints and his family. So he took badly to the first year being out of work and I just jollied him along. And then he found his new role. He does what he can in the house. I'm not a perfectionist anyway so he looks after me now. And it's funny, I come in from work and I hear him talking to the kids like a mum: 'Get them plates from downstairs' and, 'You should be doing this,' and 'You haven't got your homework done.' And he'll say, 'God, I'm pleased you're home, the kids have been driving me round the bend!' And I think, 'God, that's what our mam used to say to our dad!'

We've swapped roles a bit but we're both comfortable with it now.

Elaine Brettle, age 43
Middlesbrough

Make a Joke

When I'm talking to people now, I say, 'Well, I've been married four times and they all died happy.' I never give them the gruesome bits! And the man over there says, 'They all died with a smile on their faces, Peggy.'

I say, 'Yes, that's it.' I make a joke of it. I don't tell them the heartache. I forget about that.

Margaret Greaves, age 86
Thornaby

CHAPTER 6

A bit of wangling

Some things that used to be acceptable are now frowned upon. Some things that invoked the wrath of the law seem surprisingly harmless now. We decided to look at some of the 'grey areas', to find out where the boundaries of acceptability have been for different generations and what happened if people overstepped the mark.

A policeman with a group of men outside a public house or wine merchant in Middleton in Teesdale. (Beamish. The North of England Open Air Museum, Co. Durham)

William and Mary Wigston at home, Hamsterley, Co. Durham, 1957. Mr Wigston had been a policeman in Gateshead after the First World War. (Bill Wigston)

Drink and Drive

You can't drink and drive nowadays, can you? I took my mother and father to the pictures at Bishop and we had a lodger from Newcastle who was working on the forestry then; and we popped into this pub and how the hell I got my mother and father home, I don't know. I was going to a dance – it was a Friday night and I was going to a dance – and the garage was down the bottom fields then. I said, 'I'm going.' My father said, 'You're not! You're in no fit state.' I said, 'I'm going!' I got out the car and disappeared in the gutter…couldn't get out the gutter, so I wasn't in any fit state!

I didn't know how or what road I came home that night. I thought, 'That's stupid.' But of course, there wasn't as much traffic on the road in them days and the cars wouldn't go as fast – fifty mile an hour, or sixty, was about as fast as it would go. And there was no breathalyser in those days, you know.

Tommy Hilton that lived in the farmhouse, he used to go out to Howden le Wear, which is about ten mile away, and he used to drink and you couldn't pass him on the road because he was hitting both sides of the kerb…he was hitting one verge and then the other side…and he never had an accident. He drove for thirty years and never – how the devil he got away with it, I don't know. But there wasn't a policeman either.

Bill Wigston, age 69
Hamsterley, Bishop Auckland

Gambling

Like all mining villages, there was a lot of gambling on very minor things. I mean, one of the common things was a game called 'pitch and toss', where you throw up two pennies into the air and you bet on whether it's coming down heads, tails, whatever. Well, this went on every weekend on the fells. You could see men drifting across the fells gradually and you could see the number gradually growing and growing, and in some depression in the hills they would get together and they would be gambling on the pitch and toss. Now, this was illegal so the police were constantly raiding these groups. So to try and head this off they used to pay men a few pennies to sit on the hilltops to act as lookouts. 'Jim Crows', they called them, on the lookout for the bobbies coming. And of course, if they spotted a bobby coming they would yell and suddenly all these men would be running in all directions. Rumour has it there was always somebody left behind to grab the money and pocket it and take off.

Harry Peart, age 71
Darlington

Local Bookie

Eventually, our local bookie retired. And he was a grand fellow. He was landlord for so long…anyway, this day, Archie would finish. 'Does tha want to take over, Fred?' He says 'Aye.' 'Well,' he says, 'You'll have to borrow some money. You'll need a stake.' So he went to my granddad and he staked him. And he won a few bob, he did, and so he started bookie-ing. And they brought their bets to the house, and some of them only put sixpence each way, and one lady threepence each way every day and loved it. Loved it.

It was just starting to come in then where you must not book-keep in your house. You mustn't run a book. But he never got caught. And he also run football coupons. They weren't quite…it wasn't too bad an offence at that point but still, I don't think it was all that legal. But we got a telly, we got all sorts.

He also run the local sweep, and during the war he handed out the tea and sugar. All miners got so much tea and sugar. Well, we never went short of tea and sugar because he always fiddled a bit for us! We had best tea and sugar all through t' war!

He'd give 'em it, my dad, he wouldn't take it from them. He'd give 'em it. I think he might have put down there was four hundred when there was three hundred. I don't know. Because they all got a bit extra, not only him of course. He did a bit of wangling, that's it. That's it.

Norma Templeman, age 61
North Skelton

Apples and Turnips

Living in a rural community, you would steal apples, you would steal turnips from the field and things and, you know, that was going on all the time. But if you were caught, of course, it was another matter because everyone knew who you were!

Harry Peart, age 71
Darlington

Fair Game

You have a farmer who probably has several fields full of turnips and potatoes. They're the things people need to survive. And so that's fair game – take a few potatoes out of a field, or a few turnips, that's fair game. I'm not saying it's fair game but I think that was the attitude. But they wouldn't steal a turnip from each other, for instance. I don't think that would happen at all. I think anything else, anything that belonged to – well, perhaps no-one in particular. I mean, who does a pheasant belong to? Who does a rabbit belong to? Look at it that way. I think that's the way they looked at it, quite frankly.

Colin Berwick, age 66
Brotton

Poachers

My husband, Tommy Templeman, and his mate, Billy Lancaster, were two of the best poachers round here. My husband hated work, but I lived like a lord. I was sick to death of trout, pheasant, grouse, duck – mallard, fresh fish from the sea. I was fed up to the teeth of it.

They weren't greedy poachers. They were never going up with a sack and filling a sack of pheasants. Never. Every poacher – and there was quite a few –

The buffer repair shop, British Railways Workshops, Shildon, March 1964. (John Collinson)

was never greedy. He'd get his one or a brace and I don't know any miner or anybody who ever got more than that.

Norma Templeman, age 61
North Skelton

Firewood

I can remember, again as a boy, the miners used to come out from front shift at about two o'clock time, something like that, and walk down the street and they invariably wore macintoshes. And these macs had huge pockets on the inside. And they would push lumps of wood – large lumps, clogs – clogs of wood in there. Now, that wasn't stealing as such because very often those pieces of wood would have been pit props. But when they reached a point where they were unsafe, when a new prop had to be put in for instance,

the old prop had to be taken to the surface and put in a heap somewhere, and I should imagine the miners would…there'd be a fellow up there with a saw, wouldn't there? And he would saw it up into pieces and they would go and help themselves and take it home for firewood.

Colin Berwick, age 66
Brotton

Perk of the Job

The railway always did fair with me and I always did fair with them. They were very fair with me. I never did anything – apart from a few nails or a little bit of wood in my pocket, like. But nothing serious, no. It was just a perk of the job, that. A few screws and a few nails.

To me, on the railway, the biggest crime

65

up there, in my opinion, was pinching brass. And I'll tell you an incident about a bloke. Just up the other end of the town there's a big bank. He had a little horse and a little flat cart, some straw. The horse was plodding up this bank, sweating like a little horse. When he was stopped, the bloody cart was full of brass! Railway brass. Aye, he got caught. Finished.

John Collinson, age 75
Shildon

No Evidence

One Christmas, with my husband being out of work – he wasn't out of work, he just didn't like to go – we hadn't a fowl. So they went all round the allotments and they thought, 'Oh, he's loaded with fowl there. We'll have one of his.' So they did. They went out, that night. And I'd been crying, saying, 'There's no bird for us on Christmas Day.' And we'd had a row because he wouldn't work and I was working, doing two jobs to keep us going. And he went out and he got this fowl, this chicken. Ploated it in the house. Of course, we had a beautiful open fire, burnt all the feathers. And not only that, he'd pinched half a dozen eggs and all.

'Now,' I says, 'they'll know you've got it!' 'Yes,' he says, 'I know they will. But I'll put that right with my fellow man.'

What happened, I don't know, but t' lad knew – he knew somebody – but he didn't know Tom had got that chicken. He didn't know. And he went straight to the police about it. And PC…I don't think it was PC

Durham then…I forget who the copper was, but he'd make a few inquiries. There was no evidence.

Norma Templeman, age 61
North Skelton

Ashamed

There was this inherent morality within a village community – it wasn't written down – but the code of honour, the code of morality, was extremely strong. So you would be shamed if you were caught out doing something wrong. I mean, when I first started school I went from the first class into the second class and the second class, the lady's name – I remember the teacher – Mrs Thomson. And we had free milk, and they had a biscuit tin and of course you got this free milk and she would hand out a biscuit. Now, I remember, with another boy, creeping into the classroom one time and finding the biscuit tin and helping ourselves to the biscuits.

We were caught. Now first of all, we were severely punished. This teacher had a huge – it wasn't even a cane, it was a sort of pole from a map that used to hang on the wall. It had a metal rod going down the middle and a thick thing. So you got several whacks over the outstretched hand with this. But in addition, of course, you were hauled off to see the headmaster and then you would be publicly paraded. He would take you round every classroom and tell the rest, every class, what you had done. So this was a kind of 'naming and shaming,' as it were.

And if your parents got to know, not only would they be shamed but you'd get another good hiding at home. You'd get walloped again for what you'd done at school.

Harry Peart, age 71
Darlington

On and On

I was driving about in pinched cars when I was ten. At first, when I first started pinching, I reckon I started off, like, shoplifting and pinching car signs off the cars and stuff. It just went from there, like. From the car signs to doing the doors or smashing the windows and raking about inside and taking the cassettes. It just went on and on from there.

Paul Robinson, age 20
HMYOI Deerbolt, Barnard Castle

Robbery

There wasn't professional violence, villain against policeman, to the same extent. About 1961, robbery was

Bishop Auckland police station, High Bondgate. (Beamish. The North of England Open Air Museum, Co. Durham)

not a very common offence, even in the metropolis. And I went on early turn at Chelsea as a PC in 1961 and, along with five others, were picked out and sent to Fulham. This is six o'clock in the morning. And at Fulham, we were allocated, each of us, a prisoner. And I was taken into a cell at Fulham and handcuffed to a man. And I was to take him, in the police van, handcuffed, to West London Magistrates Court. I'll never forget it as long as I live. It was a man called Shaw.

The day before, Shaw and his five mates had robbed the London Underground wages office at Lots Road, had gone in with baseball bats and shotguns, smashed everything, pole-axed about twenty people and stolen the wages. And the Flying Squad arrested them. And they were going to West London Court. And they were seen to be so violent that they had to be handcuffed to a PC each. So I was handcuffed to this man, Shaw. He has glasses on, horn-rimmed glasses. And he got up and he never stopped coming up. He was enormous! He was about six foot four, big man – he wasn't fat – he was a big man.

So out we go to the van. In the van, West London from Fulham was about two and a half miles. Got out the van, into the cells – the court cells at West London. At that stage the handcuffs were taken off and I said, 'Thank God for that!' And Shaw said, "What do you mean?' I said 'You could have just picked me up and put me through the wall of the van, you're so big.' 'I wouldn't do that', he said.

I said, 'Yesterday, you flattened about six people with a baseball bat.'

He said, 'That was work.' That's an absolutely true story. Shaw said, 'I would never do any harm to you.' And as far as I know, he meant it.

Jack Ord, age 67
Middlesbrough

Fighting

I was in a small school and there was this chap, Oswald Cairns – he's since died, he was older than me. And his brother was about my age and we must have had a fight, because in these Irish Catholic schools they were always fighting – or they were in them days – so I was fighting him and he got his big brother. Well, my father always told us if there was more than one I could use whatever I had so I did – I kicked him. And I kicked him down, the big lad, you see. And then I hammered his brother. So after dinner his mother was at the school to the headmistress and, 'What's all this, Willy?' and I told her, I said, 'Well, my father told us if there was more than one – and his big brother was there so I had to deal with him first and I did…' And then she said, 'Oh, is that it, then? Go back to your classroom.' She understood the code.

Bill Wigston, age 69
Hamsterley, Bishop Auckland

Bullying

When I worked in the shipyard there was a striker there and he had hands that were that big – they were like a shovel. And I always remember he didn't like me because he used to work for our old man when he was foreman and he'd put this fellow down a couple of times for bullying and what have you. And any chance he had of having a go at me I got this great big hand shoved in my face, you know. Anyway, the old man, he did put him down. He picked him up by his throat one day – I mean, he'd be about eighteen stone – he just picked him up by his throat and held him up in the air. He said, 'If you've had enough just tell me and I'll put you down.'

He never really smacked anybody, he just...you know, he'd either get a grip of them and squeeze them or just bounce them. I never really saw him give anybody a good smack.

Peter Kitchen, age 60
Stockton

Knives

If somebody is going to hammer you, you fight back. You don't allow them to knock you flat because, I mean, they'll just kick you if you get down nowadays. In them days, nobody would get out a knife to stick you. That was a terrible day if anybody showed a knife like that – pooh! You would shun them. You wouldn't have nothing to do with 'em.

Bill Wigston, age 69
Hamsterley, Bishop Auckland

Fists

It was fists. So they ended up with a black eye or a broken jaw and you ended up with all your knuckles skinned. But that didn't matter. That healed quite all right.

Norma Templeman, age 61
North Skelton

Rage

I can go into, when I was young, into – I think it was like the Vikings – like a sort of a rage in which I couldn't see, couldn't see or hear – and then, after it was all over, my mates used to tell us what had happened.

Bill Wigston aged eighteen, in Egypt, 1947. (Bill Wigston)

I must have been about fifteen or maybe sixteen. And we were going to the pictures and we were just a bit late for the first house. It was a pit village and we went through this wood, and there was an opening in the wood and there was eight chaps and one of them was older than us, like. Whether he'd been in the Army or whether he was in the pits I don't know. And we were all about the same age except him. And soon as I saw them I realised there was trouble and my stomach seemed to knot up.

Anyway, there was just this little meadow in the wood and there was a wicket gate and I thought we were going to get out of it because I could have outrun these two but you can't run away from trouble with your mates.

One jumped on my mate Matty, and then there was four and they were standing on like a little ridge and furrow and they were standing a bit above me. I'm thinking to myself, 'Now, I'll say something, like, witty, or something' you know, but it was taken out of my hands because one of them hit us with a stick across the nose and there's blood all over. And I didn't know anything more until all of a sudden I heard, like, screaming going on and then there was like this pink mist. I came out this pink mist and it was this big 'un. I had a hold of him by the hair but I was in slow-motion, and my fist was going into him and he was screaming his head off and then I thought, 'Right!' so I put the boot in. You know, shoes, of course. It couldn't hurt that much. Matty Barnes told me I just waded into them and was chucking these fellows all over the place!

And it's happened once or twice, which is dangerous. So after that, when I come out the Army, I thought to myself 'Now, if you can stay clear of trouble, stay clear of trouble.' Because I could have done some damage.

Bill Wigston, age 69
Hamsterley, Bishop Auckland

Bill's childhood friend, Matty Barnes, 1947. (Bill Wigston)

CHAPTER 7

Growing up

Not just about the innocence of childhood, 'Growing up' is about a long line of hurdles to be cleared in the race for adulthood. Surviving infancy, going to school, the eleven plus examination, boyfriends and girlfriends, rebellion, starting work, leaving home and getting married are all part of the process.

Lawson Street School, Middlesbrough, 1907. Standing at the back is the headmaster, Mr Hanks, who later became headmaster at Marton Grove School. (Bert Ward)

Too Soon

My twin sister and I were born two months too soon, and my mother didn't even know she had twins. I was born and then my twin sister came ten minutes later. She'd had all the food and I wasn't expected to live. I was like a very skinny rabbit, my mother said.

They put cotton wool in a shoebox and put me near a fire. I was too young to suckle so my mother had to fill a fountain pen with milk and put it in my mouth drop by drop. And that first day, the midwife came four times: 'Is it dead yet?'

Margo Coser, age 68
Hartlepool

Diptheria

I can remember – with a certain amount of sadness, actually – the last Christmas my younger brother was alive. He died in 1934 with diphtheria. We were living in Dormanstown, in Cleveland Place. The last Christmas would, of course, be 1933. I would be five, just started Dormanstown School. He, in fact, got a conductor's set. Probably people won't know what that was – it was a little cap and a little ticket machine. And I actually got a clockwork train that went on a circular route – it didn't have any straight lines. And I can always remember he was most unhappy and disgruntled at the fact that he wanted this railway set. And I can see him now, sitting in the middle of it, more or less

Margo Coser (*née* Hutchinson), left, with her twin sister Sybil, around 1930. (Margo Coser)

commandeering this particular engine set and it going round and round and round him. And I had to sit on the outside. And I always remember my mother and dad saying, 'Oh, well, let him have a play with it.' You know.

Harry Foster, age 70
Northallerton

Devastated

I was just getting ready to go out to school when the telegram came – you got a telegram. I was just devastated, because for all he was six years older than I was we'd always been great friends, you know. I remember thinking then, 'I'll never let anything hurt me again. I'll never care for anybody again. I'll always make sure that nothing ever matters to me because I can never be hurt like this again.' And I consciously, as a young person, made that decision that nothing would ever hurt me like that again. I was completely devastated.

Joyce Raine, age 72
Bishop Auckland

Coronation Souvenir

I remember the beginning of the century, Queen Victoria had been on the throne since 1837 and she died in 1901. And she was succeeded by Edward VII. That was in 1901 but it was not until 1902 that the Coronation took place. I remember it very well indeed. I had three sisters older than I was, and they were at school. And each schoolchild was given a memento or a souvenir of the Coronation. And on this particular day they all came running home with their little souvenirs to my mother, all agog. There was such a bustle in the house that I couldn't get a word in edgeways.

The souvenir was in the shape of a tin box, about four inches by two by a half an inch, and inside, wrapped in silver paper, was a piece of chocolate. And I looked all agog, all in astonishment. And I pulled my mother's frock and I said, 'Where's my chocolate?'

And she says, 'You don't go to school yet. They're only given to schoolchildren. Next year you'll be four,' – I was three at the time – 'You'll be four and you'll go to school.' And that was what I had to live with!

Joseph Dickinson, age 100
Hartlepool

Responsibility

I think I got the first key to the front door when I was eight and I used to come in from school, at eight years old; I can remember distinctly my mother would be running the office of the driving school and my father would be out teaching people to drive. So I would tend to come in and set the fires and light the fires and start to prepare a meal.

Lionel Danby, age 55
Carlton, Stockton-on-Tees

Bill Wigston (back row, far right) in Indian headdress, c. 1938. His friend Matty Barnes is in the tent, holding a cauliflower. (Bill Wigston)

Religious Education

They used to teach you just as much as they had to teach you, you know. And, of course, a lot of the education where I went to was religious education. Your catechism and all that, because the priests say, 'Give me the child 'til he's about six or seven and I'll give you the man.' And they do. But it doesn't do very much for your education later on. No damn good at all! You know, 'Who made you? God made me. Why did He make you? He made me to love Him, honour Him and serve Him…' A load of utter rubbish!

Bill Wigston, age 69
Bishop Auckland

Expectations

In 1943 the eleven plus was operating in those days and it was called the scholarship. I was fortunate enough to win a scholarship, or pass the examination and go to the grammar school. And my brother, he passed an exam at thirteen and went to a technical school. So I think my mother's horizons suddenly became wider because of that. I don't remember her putting a lot of pressure on us to do a particular thing. But I think there was an expectation there that we wouldn't sort of end up as labourers or whatever.

Colin Berwick, age 66
Brotton

74

Destiny

I didn't pass the eleven plus. If you passed the eleven plus and you went to the grammar school, you were destined to be either a school teacher or – you know, that was the course. If you went to the secondary school, you were destined to be, if you were top in the secondary school, a clerical worker or down to the factory workers but you knew where your place was even at that stage.

And something else that I can remember which, I mean, they would cringe at today, the Women's Libbers. My mother and father, as I say, they were pretty open-minded, but when I didn't pass the eleven plus they said, 'Oh, it doesn't matter, you're a girl.'

Dorothy Peacock, age 60
Wheatley Hill

Rules

The first day I went to high school my mom said, 'Right. Don't eat meat, don't speak to boys.' That was it.

Shada Khan, age 32
Middlesbrough

Forty Per Cent

I never used to enjoy reading this fictitious material. I suppose there always had to be a purpose to my reading. I think this is what it was. All your English literature books, I didn't make a lot of headway with them. I'll always remember the English master –

he was a proper gentleman – he got hold of me and he tweaked my ear, and he said, 'I wish you would take some more interest in this English literature.' He says, 'You probably don't like it, but the pass mark in the examination is only forty per cent. In English grammar, mathematics, physics,' he says, 'you will easily achieve vastly more than forty per cent. Do you not think you can settle down and at least try to achieve forty per cent?' 'Hmm,' I thought, 'well he's a reasonable fellow and he only wants forty per cent,' The others wanted a hundred. So with that reminder from him I actually did get a GCE in English literature!

Neil Pattinson, age 57
Daddry Shield, Weardale

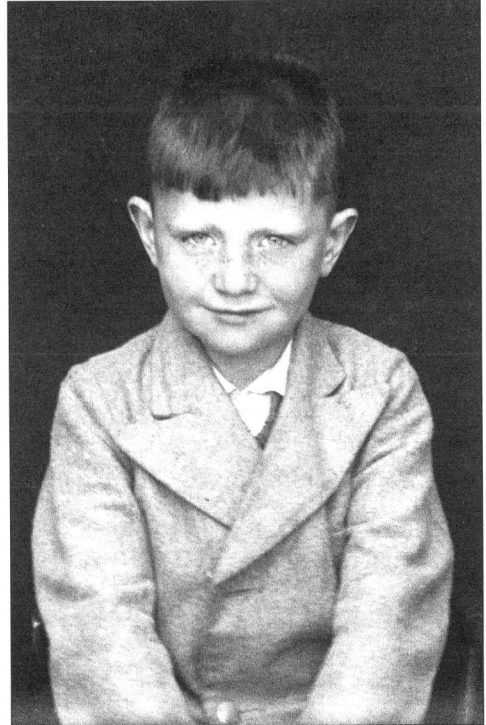

A school photograph of Colin Berwick, c. 1940. (Colin Berwick)

Dalton Village School 'Big Class', 1949. Children from the villages of Newsham, Dalton, Gayles and Kirby Hall. From left to right, back row: Dennis Leonard, Barry Teasdale, Arthur Patterson, Eric Fletcher, Bertha Plews, Moira Scruton. Second row: Eileen Webb, Ruby Cox, Heather Lowes, Hazel Braithwaite, Greta Scruton. Third row: Thomas Scruton, Joan Leonard (now Foster) Lilian Darwin, Moira Kennedy, Brian Nelson, John Leonard. Front row: Reg Dent, Dennis Coates, Thomas Barry, Arthur Blackburn. (Joan Foster)

On The Railways

I stayed at school until I was fourteen. I was eventually hounded out of school because I put my name down to go on the railways and I'd had an examination and I was accepted but there wasn't a post available. So I kept going to school until the headmaster said, one day, 'You can't come any longer.' I enjoyed it so much! He said, 'You must leave!'

Well, fortunately, that particular day I met a lad who was working on the Co-operative Stores milk. And he said, 'We're short of a lad. Will you come and work with us?' I said yes, but I was only on a fortnight and the railway sent for me. I started as a lad porter on Darlington railway station, 1936.

Ron Davies Evans, age 77
Darlington

Away to Work

Those that were clever, they didn't have much choice. They just sort

76

of finished school and started taking the pennies in. The girls would go away down country and work in the big houses and to be servants. Yes. And they would come home now and again on a holiday. And they'd be so different to what they were when they went away. Because they'd grown, and they'd been able to clothe themselves better. If they belonged to a big family, which was understandable. And we could see how well they would do and they seemed to be happy. And they wanted to go back. And some stayed away, and grew up and married wherever they settled.

Janet Jackman, age 77
Newton Aycliffe

Immaturity

I think I would probably be quite immature until I was about fifteen, sixteen, to be quite honest. You know, immature even compared to children in those days. As I say, fifteen, sixteen, I started to get more clothes-conscious and think about boys and all the rest of it. I went wild after that!

Madeleine Stott, age 41
Bishop Auckland

It's Not Done

I just refused to – not that I was necessarily rebelling, but I refused to conform. 'Why should I do that because everybody else is doing it?' And one phrase that my mother, and I think my grandmother, used to use, was, 'It's not done!' And I thought, 'What do you

mean, it's not done? If I do it, it'll be done so what…' you know, and it's, I just think, the most stupid, illogical expression. 'Why, why have I got to. Why, why?' Not that I wanted to do something that was totally against the law. I mean, I didn't want to, at the age of ten, smoke cigarettes on the bottom deck of the bus or anything like that, but I didn't want to do something just because somebody said I had to do it. 'I don't have to do it at all. I don't want to do it. I'm not going to do it.'

Patricia Tricker, age 51
Bedale, North Yorkshire

Going away to work: John Collinson (left) aged fourteen at Queensbury Brickworks, Bradford in 1938. Who says children grow up more quickly today? (John Collinson)

Abundance

Teenagers rebel in any case. But when you've had nothing and then everything's given to you…I mean, after the '50s and after the war, phew! Jobs, anything you wanted, was in abundance. You were bound to rebel a little bit.

I can always remember going to Wheatley Hill dance and seeing the first Teddy Boys and they were all dressed in their long coats. My husband was a Teddy Boy, he had a long green coat with the velvet collar. And we were, we were rebellious. But we loved it and we would rock and roll and dance. So that's why I never held my lads back. I think, you know, I can remember what I was like at their age, you know, and I can remember what we did!

Dorothy Peacock, age 60
Wheatley Hill

By 1970 Bari and his brother Araf (right) sported long hair and the latest fashion in flared trousers. The car is Bari's too. (Araf Chohan)

Express Yourself

I was a Mod, growing up. I don't think you realise it at the time, but it becomes an expression of intent – of the way that your life will be led. Having a clean-cut, nice, gabardine suit, short hair, tie, was an expression of – certainly antithesis to people five years earlier in reefer jackets, ice-blue jeans with hooped t-shirts and sweaters who had an antithesis toward the Teddy Boys with the long drape jackets and whatever. So certainly, our time, the fact that you were either – the two great extremes were either the Greasers with their motorbikes and the Mods with their scooters. I was lucky enough, I fell off a scooter very early on so I wouldn't ever ride it and bought a car at seventeen. But it was an expression of your taste in music, your dress, a culture. Sub-culture.

Bari Chohan, age 49
Sedgefield

Smoking

I was about seventeen when I started to smoke and when I did start, the first cigarette that anybody has I think they think, 'Oooh!', now you were doing something you thought was a bit risky. I was at a girls' school and we all smoked.

Margery Lonsdale, age 59
Wearhead, Co. Durham

Wheatley Hill All Saints Youth Club Folk Group, late 1960s. From left to right, back row: Tommy Hodgson, Pauline Nicholson. Middle row: Jean Oliver Margaret Carr (now Hedley). Front row: Robert Waites, Derek Ayre. (Margaret Hedley)

Sheltered Life

I met people who I suppose to some extent shocked us. When we'd come from such a background as Wheatley Hill where you never met anyone who was wanting to stand up and be counted. And two girls in particular, when we got to Peterlee Technical College, who spring to mind and, you know, these two were outrageous and quite exciting to the rest of us because you just didn't know what they were going to do next. And I had never met anyone like that before, who would dare not turn up to a lecture, or, you know, be cheeky to the teacher in front of everyone. And it was something simple like that. But, of course, these two were into alcohol, they were into drugs, and

they were just completely alien to anything I'd ever known before. And I think it was that time when I realised, 'God, haven't I led a sheltered life!'

Margaret Hedley, age 45
Durham

Cool

And then we used to go to the Purple Onion every Saturday afternoon. Not the current Purple Onion, but the same people who ran it then. It's long since demolished now. It was a coffee bar – it was dead cool. I felt ever so trendy. I felt great going there. I used to go there and then I used to go and put a bet on at the bookie's round the corner, and maybe

79

stay the evening, have a few pints in the Corporation and various other Middlesbrough pubs.

And there was a place called The Scene, where we used to dance with donkey jackets on. That's right, all the lads used to wear donkey jackets, with hands in their pockets, and dance up and down. This is when dancing separated, you know when the sexes separated for dance. It was sort of mid-1960s. Big mistake. Big mistake! So, yeah, dancing with our hands in the pockets of our donkey jackets. Well, what a farce!

Vin Garbutt, age 52
Loftus

Ron Davies-Evans, RAF cadet, 1942. (Ron Davies-Evans)

Self-sufficient

Because of the situation we were in at home, where my mother took ill at one time and I had to do a lot of the housework, I was used to looking after myself. And I'd been working on the railways, on shift work and it wasn't too easy a job. I joined the Air Force and started training and I had the life of Riley, I thought. Because we use to get up on a morning, your breakfast was all prepared for you. The railways were making my pay up to what I'd been earning. I had a good uniform, and to adapt to that situation was so easy for me. Making my own bed and things like that. I could do my own sewing because every airman got a 'housewife' with needles and cotton and things like that. That didn't trouble me to do anything like that. Making my bed didn't. But there was some lads who had had everything done for them and they did find it difficult. I used to say to some of them, 'Well, why didn't you bring your mother with you?'

Ron Davies Evans, age 77
Darlington

White Slave Trade

I remember when I first was going down to London on my own, to start my training in the different hospitals, I remember my mother being horrified: 'Now you won't speak to anybody.' It was all the white slave trade then, and she was quite convinced I would get off the train…she said, 'It's not men that approach you, it's women you know, and they're so kind to you but that's what they're after…' and I'm sure she thought I was going to be sold into the white slave industry. I suppose each generation has it's own fears. Of course, I went to London, nobody spoke to me, you know. I was perfectly safe!

Joyce Raine, age 72
Bishop Auckland

Adolescence

I must have been about sixteen, I think…didn't really get on with my father. I didn't not like him – just because I was an adolescent I suppose, wanted to do something different. And at that time it was very, very easy to go and get yourself a flat. And at that time the local authorities would, you know, provide money for you to put yourself up in a flat. I used to still go back home, walk down the street – so did the other two lads – and go back to their parents' houses and get a good, square meal at least five times a week, if not seven – you know what I mean?

David France, age 33
Darlington

Naivety

I remember once going to Catterick Garrison hospital. I worked there for a little while before I got a job in the technical library. They used to take us in a truck on a morning from the ATS camp down to the Garrison hospital and as you drove in there was a compound on the left with all these fellows standing behind it. And as we girls

Veronica Twidle at Richmond, aged eighteen, c. 1940. (Veronica Twidle)

passed our ATS officer would say, 'You don't look in there.' And we'd say 'Why not?' 'I'll tell you when we get in.' And they were all going 'Yoohoo!' like this, you know, waving at you. And it was only when we got into the actual office that she told us it was all VD cases.

I'd never heard of anything like that. My sister was older than me, I mean, she's five years older – she knew. And, I mean, we had lesbians in the camp. I didn't know what that was. I thought it was something to do with thespians, you know, same thing. But it just shows, I mean, I was naive then.

Veronica Twidle, age 76
Saltburn-by-the-Sea

Babies

I went to work on a farm and the farmer said to me, 'Now we have a girl here called Margaret and she's had a baby to somebody,' and the man had gone away and left her. I always remember, she was doing the hearth and I was taking water out and I said, 'Well, how did the baby come out?' And I'm seventeen.

'The same bloody way as they went in!' she said. And I was aghast. I was appalled. I said, 'Oh, my God!' And that was thrown upon me like that. They never told you in school about those things.

Margaret Greaves, age 86
Thornaby

Boyfriends

The first boyfriend I had was just before my fifteenth birthday and he went to Stockton Grammar School and he was three years older than me. And I didn't choose him, he chose me – just came round our house one night and said will you go out with me, sort of thing, you know. I'd seen him around but I didn't know him. I wasn't particularly keen on him at first, he was just somebody to go out with. I think I was sort of flattered because I hadn't had a proper boyfriend before. And some of my friends had by then. Not all of them, but some of them had. But I hadn't had a proper boyfriend. I'd been to the pictures with one but only because his friend wanted to take my friend to the pictures and they sat holding hands, but this one I went with

actually fell asleep. So, you know, that was the only sort of bloke I'd been out with.

Patricia Tricker, age 51
Bedale, North Yorkshire

Grown Up

The first four years of our marriage we didn't have a house so we had to live in with family. So you couldn't sort of be right, proper, then. You were still under somebody else, sort of, sharing somebody else's fireside. But it was your lot, so you made the best of it.

Put up with a lot as well! It was the first time I ever dared to speak back to my mother. Yes. I had to do that because she thought I was still a lass and under her bidding and I had to let her know that wasn't true any more.

Janet Jackman, age 77
Newton Aycliffe

CHAPTER 8

Cousin Jack

Opinions differed as to whether traditional English cooking was ever much good. There certainly doesn't seem to be very much of it going on, especially among younger people. Now cooking seems to be a leisure activity as much as a life skill. So we thought we might preserve at least one recipe in the archive.

Underground at North Skelton ironstone mine, c. 1940. Miners came from all over the United Kingdom to work in ironstone and coal pits in the North East. Hence, a Cornish recipe became a mainstay for the Templeman family. (Beamish. The North of England Open Air Museum, Co. Durham)

Cornish Jack

My father-in-law was a miner and he worked down North Skelton pit. There was nothing more he liked than to come home to a 'Cousin Jack'. A Cousin Jack, the name itself came from his granny Templeman who lived down Richard Street, but originated from Cornwall. And she came up here for her men folk to work down the pit. And it was a 'Cornish Jack'. But when she came up here it obviously wasn't a Cornish Jack. So she called it Cousin Jack, and that is what it's called to this day.

Norma Templeman, age 61
North Skelton

Good Food

There wasn't the temptations to eat some of the rotten stuff that we get served up as food now. For instance, if a woman bought bread, the finger was pointed at her, 'She buys bread!' you know, and they all baked their own bread. And home-baked bread and butter – butter was the thing for health. Anybody that had 'maggie', well, they had maggie not by desire to slim or what have you, it was because you couldn't afford butter.

I was always into trouble with my mother because if I had jam on my bread, I liked jam on dry bread. I didn't like butter with it. Oh, no, you

'She buys bread!' Jackson's Ideal Bakery at Shildon, 1906. (Beamish. The North of England Open Air Museum, Co. Durham)

A traditional butcher's shop at Barnard Castle. Note the delivery bike with a basket. (Beamish. The North of England Open Air Museum, Co. Durham)

had to have butter, you know.

We never used to eat much more than beef – very rare that we touched pork. Mutton was fairly commonplace. There was no waste as we know a lot of waste now. Leftovers – mashed potatoes and meat – the meat would be done on the grater and made into rissoles, which were good and nourishing and a variety. My mother used to bake, not only the bread that we've mentioned but a variety of cakes. A birthday was never missed – there was always a spiced cake for birthday and Christmas and New Year.

Chicken – occasionally we had chicken because one of my dad's pals at work used to keep chickens and we would get a young one, and that was given to fatten up for Christmas and became a pet – and usually used to be swapped for somebody that was

keeping chickens so that they kept it and we ate somebody else's. We couldn't bring ourselves to kill our own!

Walter Nunn, age 78
Shildon

Local Butcher

The cut of beef that would make up this mince from your local butcher would be shin, mainly. It could be the stewing steak, but mainly the shin, which as we all know is off the leg. It would not be minced twice as it is today.

The bacon, I would buy at that same butcher because he would bone it. He would kill the pig, he'd bone it and everything would be done by that

85

butcher. But, in the meantime, Alec Batterby might have killed a pig.

Norma Templeman, age 61
North Skelton

Nothing Wasted

There was a chap in the village, Alec Batterby, he seemed to be the man who was called in to slaughter, slaughtering the animal. He stunned it. He had a contraption that – it stuck a metal spike into its forehead and hit it with a mallet, which stunned it. Then he cut its throat.

At this point my grandmother came into the proceedings. She was in charge of the black pudding. She had a pail which she held underneath the pig's throat to catch all this blood. And she was very squeamish, was gran. She didn't like blood at all. And she had a handkerchief clasped over her nose and mouth too – because the smell was not pleasant. But she still had her job to do so she held the bucket underneath the throat and turned her head away with the handkerchief pressed over it until the thing was full. And off she tottered.

Then of course it became worse because she had to dip her hands in and get all the old bits and pieces of – whatever it is – out of the blood, you see. And she loathed that job, hated it! But nothing was wasted – I mean, this was wartime.

Colin Berwick, age 66
Brotton

Penny Ducks

People would eat things that today they'd call offal. We had pig's trotters and chitlings and brawn. And

Mr and Mrs Wigston with a pig raised for slaughter, Hamsterley, Co. Durham, 1947. (Bill Wigston)

A street party marking the Silver Jubilee of King George V and Queen Mary, Darlington, 6 May 1935. (Ron Davies-Evans)

'Penny Ducks' – there was a butcher that used to sell what they called Penny Ducks. They're like a meat ball and you could get it for a penny. And they'd put gravy on for you as well. And if you had another penny you could get a penn'orth of pease pudding. So you used to get a penn'orth of pease pudding and a Penny Duck with gravy on and that was a meal.

Ron Davies Evans, age 77
Darlington

Pastry

I know this is a tradition down Cornwall that granny Templeman would bring up with her, but we wouldn't bother about it here. Every person has a different edging to the pastry and then you know who made that pastry.

My mother-in-law would certainly, no way would she use an egg to brush a pasty – that was far too extravagant. She'd just brush it with milk, but I like to give it that nice glaze.

You had a fire oven, hadn't you? So therefore the pasty would go in and the

Milk delivery at Stillington, 1930. (Beamish. The North of England Open Air Museum, Co. Durham)

oven would have been just warmed up to be hot. Now I'm going to go and rake all the fire away so as it's in a slow oven.

Norma Templeman, age 61
North Skelton

Microwave

Microwaves I think are wonderful – although I was nervous of a microwave. I was more nervous after I put a plate in with gold rims on it and burnt it out. Just like that. Just – 'pfft' – and that was it. So I had to get a new microwave. Mind, I had it four or five years. When Harry was alive, he brought it home from the office. He bought it new and I said, 'I'm not using that. He said, 'Now just watch. Just watch this Yorkshire pudding go up like that.'

A week later, I tried making meringues and I made a meringue and it filled the whole microwave! It was hilarious when it came out – it was square! The same shape as the microwave. It was the funniest thing you've ever seen. Then it slowly went 'pheeew', it went down – but it was really funny!

Veronica Twidle, age 76
Saltburn-by-the-Sea

Beautiful Meal

My mother-in-law and my mother could judge it perfectly for when granddad Tut or Rox Burluraux, my dad, walked through that door – it was ready to come out, boiling hot.

I know Cousin Jack is a winter dinner but they liked it so much it didn't matter, and it wasn't an expensive meal, you see. This was usually a Wednesday or a Thursday meal. This is my house – I aren't speaking generally. Because the mince was one of the cheaper cuts of meat but also the most tasty. The vegetables cost nothing and so you had this great big beautiful meal, we'll say for two people, for nowadays – would be at least £2 to £2.50. But now you've got to buy your vegetables.

Norma Templeman, age 61
North Skelton

Allotment

We were never short of food because father and mother were contrivers and my dad worked the allotment so we didn't have to buy potatoes and veg. What we had would go on fruit. We did refer to keeping healthy and yes, there was consideration of keeping healthy, within the limited knowledge of those days. Eat plenty of fruit, yes. We got plenty of fruit because

Dig for Victory; an allotment campaign in Durham, 1940. (Beamish. The North of England Open Air Museum, Co. Durham)

we didn't have to buy veg. Lettuce, scallions, all that kind of thing, my dad grew.

Walter Nunn, age 78
Shildon

Ice Cream

When things started to come back of course, you queued for hours. For bananas and ice cream, because ice cream was out during the war. So when the first ice cream parlour opened – I can remember the one at Norton, near what was the cinema, the Modern at that time and then it became a night club, the Fiesta – the ice cream parlour there, there used to be queues right down that road on a Sunday to get ice cream.

Of course, when fruit came back it was absolutely – we were amazed. And you found out where it was and went and queued and got it. But then things became very plentiful and variety became the name of the game with food.

Harry Davies, age 68
Billingham

Walter Willson's shop at Norton on Tees. (Beamish. The North of England Open Air Museum, Co. Durham)

Chips

One of my jobs as a kid, when I lived in Pearson Street, the Sturdys used to live next door to us and they had horses and carts and removals. And they had a big lad called Tut Fleming who worked for them, and Harry Sturdy, he had donkeys and ponies on the beach years later but they had this business. And every Friday Mrs Sturdy used to get me – I used to nip home from school and get home about five past twelve, and straight down to the Lobster Road fish and chip shop to get a tuppenny fish and two penn'orth of chips, twice, for these two lads.

Well, it's not an exaggeration, you could hardly carry them home, two penn'orth of chips. By Jove! It was – you know – you needed a net!

Harry Foster, age 70
Northallerton

Student Days

During my student days and my days in London I'd maybe meet a friend and we'd go to a Corner House. We hadn't much money then, we didn't earn much money, then, and you'd maybe go to the Corner House and have a meal, but no, nothing – you know, you'd maybe have baked beans on toast or scrambled egg on toast. But there weren't the meals that there were now available really, not to people who've just started earning, or people who were still at college and not earning, or training. I mean, while I was training I wasn't paid so it was a case of – you didn't go out and eat

more than just once as a very great treat.

Joyce Raine, age 72
Bishop Auckland

Chinese

I don't think I was quite eighteen, there was me and my friend, lifelong friend, and we had our first 'girls' night out' in Bishop Auckland. And we sat in the window seat of what was The Sportsman in the Market Place all night long. And as we were about to leave we bumped into two guys we'd gone to school with, who were going to the Chinese for a meal, and would we go with them? So we went. And I had beef…something. I think it was beef and onions with rice…and it was like lino! So yeah, great recollections of my first real foreign meal.

Madeleine Stott, age 41
Bishop Auckland

Basket Meal

I remember the first time we went out and we were having a basket meal. And these were great things, you know, a basket meal! And of course, they brought what we were having – chicken and chips or whatever – in the basket and I waited and I waited, and then I – quite innocent – I said, 'Excuse me, but we haven't got our knives and forks.'

And she sort of hooted! She said, 'No, well you're having a basket meal. The idea of a basket meal is you don't have knives and forks, but,' she said, 'I will get you them.' 'Oh no, no,' I said,

'It'll be quite all right!' Now I knew, you know, but I was quite horrified – I was just sitting there waiting for knives and forks to come.

Joyce Raine, age 72
Bishop Auckland

The Whole Lot

The pasty would be eaten when the miners came home from work. There was three shifts – front, back and nights. Front, six 'til two; back, two 'til ten; and nights, ten 'til six. He could go out with it at two o'clock or come in to it at two o'clock. If he only had half that pasty at two o'clock, when he came in at ten my husband would finish it off. If he ate the whole lot – just cook something else.

Norma Templeman, age 61
North Skelton

Eat at the Table

Meals were always all taken round the table until we got older and we were coming in at different times, either from school; my brother working and then me working, working shifts. But yes, meals were taken at the table and

North Skelton Bible Class Football Team, 1920/21. From left to right, back row: G. Beckham, G. Todd, W. Shingler, T. Templeman, W. Williams. Middle row: T. Dobinson, G. Smith, F. Symon. Front row: H. Dobinson, C. Cusby, A. Templeman, A. Claxton, I. Froud. (Norma Templeman)

List of Fixtures for 1920.

Date	Name of Club	Grd.	R'sult
Sept. 2	Guisbro' Congs....	Home	3-0
,, 18	'' ''		
,, 25	DORMANSTON	Home	4-1
Oct. 2	Brotton Wes. ...	Home	2-0
,, 9	BOOSBECK	A	1-0
,, 16	Lingdale Congs....	Away	2-2
,, 23	DUNSDALE	H	2-1
,, 30	Brotton Prims. ...	Away	1-1
Nov. 6	BROTTON CH	A	2-1
,, 13	'' ''		
,, 20	Guisbro' Prims....	Away	4-0
,, 27	~~~~		
Dec. 4	Guisbro' Church	Home	3-1
,, 11	SKINNINGROVE Home		5-0
,, 18	Boosbeck Church Away		
,, 31			

List of Fixtures for 1921.

Date	Name of Club	Grd.	R'sult
Jan. 8	DORMANSTON	A	1-0
,, 15	'' ''		
,, 22	Guisbro' Prims, ...	Home	5.0
,, 29	Brotton Prims. ...	Home	4-1
Feb. 5	Guisbro' Congs. ...	Away	3.0
,, 12	SALTBURN	H	5.0
,, 19	Lingdale Congs....	Home	3.0
,, 26	GREAT AYTON	A	3.0
Mar. 5	Brotton Wes. ...	Away	6.0
,, 12	BROTTON CH	H	6.0
,, 19			
,, 26	SKINNINGROVE	A	4.2
April 2	Boosbeck Church	Home	7.0
,, 9	DUNSDALE	A	
,, 16	Guisbro' Church...	Away	2-1
,, 23	GREAT AYTON	HOME	3.0
,, 30			

'Played 26; won 24; lost 0; drawn 2; points 50'. No doubt a Cornish Jack helped 'Tut' Templeman and his team sustain this impressive run. (Norma Templeman)

nobody left the table until they'd asked permission or had finished and left with permission to leave the table.

Walter Nunn, age 78
Shildon

Education in Food

Italian dishes: 'I'm not eating that rubbish,' they used to say. Salads: 'It's for rabbits!' Now most restaurants serve salad of some kind. But we're educated more. Still a long way to go!

George Pacitto, age 58
Redcar

A Miner's Dinner

Well now we've talked through a traditional miner's dinner but you must remember that it was granny Templeman who cooked up this idea Cousin Jack, rather than a Cornish Jack, so not everyone in North Skelton made a Cousin Jack. It's really around the Templeman family, this one.

But now you've got the ingredients why not just have a go yourself? You'll really enjoy it, you will. But don't forget, you must have thick onion gravy. Not a sauce out of a packet!

Norma Templeman, age 61
North Skelton

'Granny Templeman's Cousin Jack'

Ingredients:
Pastry made from 1lb self-raising flour; 8oz best lard, salt, water.

Filling:
A good 1lb best beef mince
2 slices bacon, cut up the same size as the beef mince
A very large potato, chopped.
A very large onion, chopped
An egg and some milk for glazing.

Method:
Salt and pepper the mince and bacon.
Roll the pastry out into a massive round, as big as you can get.
Lay the ingredients on one side of the rolled-out pastry in layers – mince, bacon, onion, potato; repeating until the filling is all used up. Add extra seasoning.
Egg the edges of the pastry; take the pastry over the filling and crimp the edges in your preferred style.
Make three cuts in the top of the pasty, about three inches long.
Put a desert spoon of water into each slit.
Brush the pasty with egg and milk.
Grease a baking sheet, place the pasty on it and place in an oven on gas mark 6.
After half an hour, or as the pasty begins to turn golden, add three more spoons of water through the cuts in the top.
Turn the oven down to gas mark 2 and cook the pasty for one to one and a half hours.
The pasty is ready when you can hear it sizzling through the slits in the top.
Serve with garden vegetables and thick onion gravy.

Recipe courtesy of
Norma Templeman

CHAPTER 9

Making ends meet

The spectre of poverty loomed over a large number of families in the North East for the first half of the century, and has never entirely gone away. Without the safety net of the welfare state, communities found other ways of keeping body and soul together. Today, most of us are richer than we might ever have imagined we could be – but at a price.

Barefoot children at Commercial Street, Middlesbrough, 1910. Scenes like this would have been familiar to Fred Morrison, born in the town in 1916. (Araf Chohan)

Financial Matters

One of the things I did as a child, with my older sister, was she loved me to tell her stories. And I used to make up stories, and one of them was about – this is going to sound really strange – one of them was about running a shop. And in the shop we would give everything to the poor people, half-penny a time. Everything cost a half-penny. Cooker, washing machine – whatever they needed they could have. And I remember thinking years later – I became a money advice worker, thinking – well, you know, that has a lot to do with what I felt that I'd actually moved into. You know, trying to be supportive in financial matters, and helping people with money matters, really.

Karen Milburn, age 41
Middlesbrough

Wage Packet

People didn't get paid in those days until Saturday afternoon. And the husband, if he got his pay, he was in the pub. And if he had any money when he came home, you were lucky.

But in those days, you see, the wife used to come down to the works. It wasn't unusual to see half a dozen wives at the works, getting the money before he came home – before he got his hands on it. They got his wage packet and she would get the money that she felt she should have before he got the rest, and the rest he would probably spend in the pub, you see.

Fred Morrison, age 82
Yarm

Every Penny

My father was a bus driver, and although he worked enormous hours to try and make sure there was always food on the table, he also was a gambler. So quite often, there wasn't food on the table. My mother's incredibly good with money. She counts every penny and she makes it work for her, but there were times when there just wasn't anything for her to work with. And I think as children we were very aware that being hungry was something that we had to deal with. And nine children – yeah, it's a lot to cope with.

Karen Milburn, age 41
Middlesbrough

Cheese and Ginger Beer

We were very hungry, so you'd snatch anything. And I remember going in one day and there was this bar of carbolic on the table. And when you rub the clothes like that it goes into a wedge. And I thought it was cheese and I took a bite. And like, she had this jug of soapy water and I thought it was ginger beer and I had a drink.

Margaret Greaves, age 86
Thornaby

Hobnail Boots

There were more kids at school in their bare feet than there were kids with boots. If it was necessary, you could get a ticket for a pair of shoes from

A Public Benefit Boot Company shop, possibly in Bishop Auckland, 1920s. (Beamish. The North of England Open Air Museum, Co. Durham)

Public Benefit. Weren't shoes, they were boots – hobnail boots – from the Public Benefit, and that's one way you got them.

People used to get shoes and sell them and things like that, you see. And it was open to that sort of thing. But there was more raggy arses in those days, you know, than anything. Everybody had a raggy arse.

Fred Morrison, age 82
Yarm

Poverty

I think I assumed it was probably true of everybody. I know as a child – I must have been about eight – I'd realised that there was a lot of misery. And I was aware of seeing tramps.

Tramps were commonplace, walking round the streets. Small children walking round the streets with no shoes on, no clothes even – just nappies. It was just…there seemed to be a greyness. In fact I saw my world, I think, as being grey at that time.

Thornaby was a very dour place, then, so I think I assumed that there was poverty – that there was a level of suffering that was just commonplace. So I don't think I ever felt that we were different.

I remember a couple of years ago, coming through Ragworth and crying on the bus because it was still there. And that was something that I certainly had thought would have been gone by the 1990s and it hadn't.

Karen Milburn, age 41
Middlesbrough

Four Bob a Week

I was four, my father died and he was a Wharfinger. We lived in a house that was four bob a week rent. And when my mother wanted something particularly bad she used to not pay the rent that week. But she had to pay double the next week.

She worked. Well, she worked at the Big Wesley, scrubbing the floors and all that sort of thing. That's what she did.

Fred Morrison, age 82
Yarm

George Edward Berwick, Colin's father, 1920s. He was in the East Yorks Regiment. (Colin Berwick)

A Way of Life

I think they'd had to find a way of earning a few bob in any way that they could. Going brambling, for instance, or mushrooming and things like that. Going for firewood. I mean, during the war we had to go for firewood. And we had to go onto the railway side and find – sometimes a train would go across, the fellows would throw coal out for you to pick up, put in your bucket and take home.

You had to eke out an existence. I'm not saying we were on our beam ends, not at all, but my dad would often come home with rabbits and so on that he'd either…acquired in some way or other. Poached, or somebody had given him one or sold him one. And that was the way of life.

Colin Berwick, age 66
Brotton

Picking Cinders

I remember the '26 coal strike very well, because we'd been in the coal business. Coal cost twelve and six a bag. Well, a lot of people used to go up cinder-picking. There was a – where the old Linthorpe potteries were, up at Linthorpe, top of Linthorpe Road – there was a big quarry where they'd taken the clay out for the potteries. And there was a firm at Cargo Fleet used to bring wagons over and put the ash from their furnaces and that in this thing. And people used to go and pick cinders there. People would go all day picking cinders. And they'd end up with a bag of cinders and that did them the week.

Mary Ferguson off to gather sea coal, photographed at Seaton Carew by the Revd James Pattison, 1900. (Beamish. The North of England Open Air Museum, Co. Durham)

Ron Hick's grandfather, William Childs, in 1937. He often exchanged vegetables from his garden for services in the village. (Ron Hick)

just us, you know. Granddad used to go and get a haircut and never pay for a haircut; go next door to the pub and get half a beer and never pay for it. He had a big garden, you see, and he was always in the garden. And if there was a surplus of apples, plums, pears, damsons, whatever – or even if they only wanted a few carrots – they only had to mention it and granddad would put it at the door for them. And I think it was a good system for their day, you know, that people were so friendly, and everybody knew everybody, you know.

Although they hadn't much money, they had a lot of collateral in the sense of good food and good neighbours and people who would do them a good turn, you know; if they wanted a bit of hay making they'd come along and give a hand. Things like that.

Ron Hick, age 72
Darlington

That and sea coal. People used to bring sea coal round the houses from places like Seaton where they could get the sea coal.

Fred Morrison, age 82
Yarm

Payment in Kind

A very understood thing in them days, which you don't get so much today, is payment in kind. This went on all over the village, of course. It wasn't

A Dozen Eggs

My mother went out wallpapering. And when she did 'Swannie's' – Mr Swan's – she got a lovely dish with a dozen eggs straight from that hen run, still warm, in that dish. And that's what she got for papering a room.

Norma Templeman, age 61
North Skelton

In the Same Boat

Everybody was in the same boat. Nobody had any better opportunities. I mean, I can remember my last year in the Coatham C of E school, one family had a car out of the whole class. Nobody I knew had a telephone. I don't think I'd ever been in a house where there'd been a telephone.

So generally speaking, you were actually part of a massive scene of people who were comparatively poor. Most fathers were out of work or working with limited opportunities. And most people, as I say, were in this same situation. So, you know, you didn't consider yourself any different.

Harry Foster, age 70
Northallerton

Help

It was you helped one another. If it hadn't have been for the neighbourliness and the help that people got from neighbours, you know, none of them would have survived.

Fred Morrison, age 82
Yarm

Kindness

I remember going to school and I never wanted to be off school. My mother would make me stay off. And I used to say, 'I'm going to tell 'em you made me stay off!' Well, this day, I only had the clothes I stood up in. So my mother would wash them. So I had to stay off. So – we felt nothing about it, you know! So when I went to school the next day, teacher's writing away; 'Why weren't you in school?' 'My mother had to wash my clothes.' And she looked up,

and she looked at me. And the next day she said to the children, 'All put your heads on your desks. Come out, Margaret Kennedy.' I went out and she'd bring me a big bundle of clothes: 'Now go home.' And I went home and just spilled them on the mat and there was clothes, you know, for everybody. Wasn't that kind of her?

Margaret Greaves, age 86
Thornaby

For Ever More

We'd applied to the council and we got a letter to say we had a prefab. So we went in a prefab. And it was like being in a castle. The fact that we had our own home at last, after all that time – about four years.

And we sort of managed to get it furnished on the HP that it was, them times. Now it's visa cards and all the rest of it, but it was different then. But we managed all right.

I bought it all at Hardy's furniture shop in Newgate Street; and Bell and Rainers in Newgate Street. And used to call in and pay what was due. Two and six, two shillings, five shillings, no limit to the months. It seemed as though you were paying for ever more because you paid for your goods and then you had interest to pay after that, see. And the interest would be twice as much as what the value was. Well, you knew all that, but then again, if you didn't go into it, you got nothing.

Janet Jackman, age 77
Newton Aycliffe

Credit

You didn't buy things on credit. We felt very guilty when we bought our first car because we had to buy that on credit, obviously. And it was just something you didn't do. I think a lot of people did – they bought clothes from the catalogues and they bought Provident tickets which meant you had ten pounds to spend and you paid for it so much a week over a period of weeks. But I'd been brought up in a family that never did that. We were Methodists and it was one of the things that wasn't acceptable to them.

Jean Kendall, age 66
Hurworth

Cash Only

One of my brothers, who still lives with my mum – and he is dead set against credit of any kind, and is very, very critical of people who use it and who use credit cards and don't pay cash on the nail. He pays cash for everything. If he gets a new car, it's cash. And, all right, he can afford to do it. But I often say, 'You know, if it hadn't been for catalogues and credit, when you were a kid, you wouldn't have had trousers to your backside. You wouldn't have had boots to your feet.' That's the only way my mum could clothe us sometimes, with the help of the catalogues, and the 'divvie' from the Co-op.

She was always very careful, mind, that she finished – or almost finished – one lot before she got anything else. She didn't run a catalogue of her own.

It was a next-door neighbour, who, incidentally, was a widow and I think she ran the catalogue and she got commission so it helped her out.

Joan Foster, age 59
Norton

Subbing

You were able to 'sub'. You know, there was a lot of subbing went off in those days. You worked for a firm but by the end of the week you didn't have any money to pick up because you'd subbed it all through the week.

And then, a lot of pawning. I mean, you pawned what you could in the pawn shop in Newport, and if you had anything to pawn you pawned it on the Monday and you got it back on the Friday. And a lot of people used to exist like that. You pawned what you could and you got four or five shillings and you lived on that a week and then at the weekend you were able to get back, redeem it. And then it went in again!

The people that lived next door to us, the husband, he hadn't worked for many years. And when he was offered a job he'd forgotten his trade.

Fred Morrison, age 82
Yarm

Worse Off

My father was sent to Wolsingham to work, and his lodgings were a shilling less than his wage. So we were worse off. And he came home one

Friday night and his face was beaming. Mother said, 'What's the matter?' He said, 'I've got the sack!' We were back on unemployment pay, you see, onto twenty-six shilling a week instead of a shilling. Those were most difficult times.

Ron Davies Evans, age 77
Darlington

Benefit System

I was married when Margaret Thatcher came into power, and my ex – now my ex-husband – was made redundant. He stopped working, I think, the year she took office, 1979. And he never worked again. So for thirteen years of our marriage he never worked. Which meant, of course, I actually brought my children up in the benefits system. So I've had first-hand experience of those years, on the wrong side of it. It taught me how to survive on very little money.

Karen Milburn, age 41
Middlesbrough

Public Assistance Committee

The biggest queues I ever saw when I was a lad were the queues round the Public Assistance Committee in Fleetham Street. People going for vouchers to get food. And in those days they give a voucher, you know. People presented themselves there and the Board of Guardians used to determine what your state of deprivation was. And they either gave you a voucher for ten bob, or if you

Ron Davies-Evans' parents, Lucy and Tom, 1930. (Ron Davies-Evans)

had a lot of children they would up it to another five bob, something like that.

The vouchers were made out for the Home and Colonial in Newport Road. And, I mean, people went along and they got their groceries. You couldn't have cigarettes or anything like that – that was taboo.

Fred Morrison, age 82
Yarm

Child Benefit

Child benefit was the luxury because benefits themselves paid for the necessities and child benefit, once a week, would buy the children a yoghurt or bits and pieces that they wouldn't normally have. So they would have a choice at that point. It used to be, 'Do you want a piece of fruit or a yoghurt?' and they used to plump for yoghurts most of the time. And maybe go to the pictures now and again.

Karen Milburn, age 41
Middlesbrough

Means Tested

When you applied to the PAC for assistance, the first thing, a man used to come round the house and see that you didn't have anything. If you had anything in the house you didn't get anything. Or you could sell anything, you didn't get anything, you see. It's like the old means test, I mean, the means test was entirely the same. If people had anything, 'Oh, sell that…sell that sideboard, you don't need it. Live on the money.'

Fred Morrison, age 82
Yarm

Stigma

The culture of being on the National Assistance, as it was then called, was a stigma. People, you know – they said, 'Oh, they're on the "Nash". They're not nice people.' In other words, they're not looking after themselves, they're not pulling their weight.

There were always unemployed people and there were always people very hard up, who had no money at all;

and therefore, as I said, this idea of charity and helping each other…but even saying the word 'charity' – people did not like charity. You know, you hadn't got to be seen to be a charity case. I mean, at school they sometimes would say, like, 'Hands up, anybody whose father's not working', you know, and if you put your hand up you were then allowed free dinners, or something. Well, to the parents that would be a great relief but you would go home and say, 'Johnny so-and-so got free dinners,' you know, and it's a kind of – you're telling about something private and personal that the villagers wouldn't want you to know, because of their pride. They wouldn't want that to be out, that they weren't paying for their school dinners or milk or whatever.

Harry Peart, age 71
Darlington

CHAPTER 10

Sheep on the runway

Rapid mass transport has been with us for the whole century, on the railways. In fact, for many years, travelling short distances was often a lot harder than travelling long distances, if the experiences of our contributors are anything to go by.

Lionel Danby's grandfather, William, at the wheel of Sir Malcolm Campbell's 'Bluebird'. William Danby was one of the team of engineers who assisted Campbell in his record-breaking land speed run at Utah in 1935. This picture was taken at Danby's Ayrsome Garage on Linthorpe Road in Middlesbrough. (Lionel Danby)

Removals

I was born at Tynehead in Cumberland and my father was a shepherd and his father before him. My father lived at a very lonely place – it's very well known, it's called Moor House – way up. It was seven miles from a village, anyway.

Well, when I was four years old he moved over to Weardale. Brotherlee, near Westgate. And that was an experience! Because they brought the furniture over the tops, right over from Alston and the horse got itself too far over the road and the furniture tipped into the ditch. And he couldn't get it up. It was just himself, you see. He had to take the horse out and go back and get another one.

Well, he walked from there, from right on those tops, down to Westernhope Burn, between Westgate and Eastgate to get somebody else to come and help him with another horse…two horses. They pulled it out.

And then he had to take a load down. He begged a night's lodgings with the boss, the new man he was going to, and then they had to come back with him and they had to get another load. And that's how they got the furniture over.

Maude Coulthard, age 84
Ireshopeburn, Co. Durham

Preferred transport: Geordie Smith and a Dales Galloway, Co. Durham, 1947. (Bill Wigston)

A Skurr's bus,
Stillington, 1930s.
The would-be driver is
Maurice Skurr.
(Maurice Skurr)

A Bike

I was living right in the country. There was a bus in the village. It went to Thirsk on a Monday, to Northallerton on a Wednesday and I think it went to both places on a Saturday. But you had to be there and you had to come back at the prescribed time. I mean, if you missed it there wasn't another one in fifteen or twenty minutes, or anything like that, and it didn't dump you at your door either.

Mother suggested that I saved my money and got myself a bike. So I did a bit of scraping and saving – not that there was much to save. I think it was about twenty-eight shillings a month I

got then. The man my mother was housekeeping for said, 'If you meet me in Thirsk on Monday afternoon, at a certain time, I'll take you down to the bike shop where you'll get a decent bike, you know, and you won't be fiddled or anything like that.' So he took me down to Hyde's little shop and I was given a catalogue to look at, a bit of advice. I settled on this BSA Roadster, it was. It was black with a little green line round it.

Living there and in those days it meant absolutely everything. You were free, when it was your day off, your afternoon off, you could go. I mean, when sometimes you hadn't anywhere to go you just spent your afternoon

107

sitting in the servant's hall or your bedroom, reading or doing your knitting or whatever you were doing, which wasn't much change from what you did anyway on an afternoon! I had more pleasure out of that bike than any single one thing I've had in my life, I think.

Sarah Jones, age 81
Stockton

Transportation

My father worked for many years as an electrician but in 1922, I think, bought a small Ford – one of the earliest Ford trucks – and started transporting goods around for anyone, anywhere, on a part-time basis. Because

this was something new, far removed from the horse and cart that had been used to that time, he met with reasonable success, I suppose. So in 1924 he bought what we knew as the Ford Grange, which was a convertible vehicle, where he could remove the coach part, which he did with the assistance of others, and it was slid off the back and stood on four oil drums whilst he took the truck away to transport goods. No doubt at the end of the day we'd come back, restore the coach and probably take twelve passengers down to Stockton.

I recall some of our buses going to Scarborough or – all around the coast, actually. And particularly to Harrogate, York, up into the Dales, up into the Durham area. But after the war, the

Going for a ride. Hannah Wallace of Richmond with two friends, *c.* 1918. (Ray Wallace Thompson)

Brenda Horness, then Pte Varty, B W/249378, a dispatch rider on a Matchless 350cc motorbike, 1945. (Brenda Horness)

hire side of it really exploded. We had all over. Particularly Blackpool and Blackpool illuminations.

Maurice Skurr, age 80
Marton

Week's Holiday

My family used to take us to Blackpool. There was one big reason for that. My father didn't suffer the best of health in his later years while he was working. He had chest complaints and he eventually died of silicosis. But when we went to Blackpool, his health improved considerably while he was there and for a while after. So our holidays were,

mainly, to go to Blackpool but we used to sometimes go to Scarborough. Now, I think that would be the extremities, geographically, of the distances that we would venture. And only for a week – well, they only got a week's holiday unpaid.

Ron Davies Evans, age 77
Darlington

Day Out

In the holiday time, the local coal people, coal merchants, used to go along to the Salvation Army. And they had these long forms in the Salvation Army. And they used to get a couple of

The Inn, Tan Hill, Swaledale. (Fremont Hutchinson)

these long forms and tie them onto the lorries – horse-drawn lorries – and they would charge you sixpence to go from Middlesbrough to Leven. Leven and back. And that was as much holiday as anybody ever had. And there would be lots of these coal carts and families going to Leven for a day out at Leven Bridge. Alternately they went to Seaton Carew. And that was their holidays.

Fred Morrison, age 82
Yarm

New Experience

We used horses when I was small. I must have been perhaps about fourteen and I was allowed to drive my father's mare to Yarm to collect something. And a little bit before we got to Yarm station, there's what they call the watering-spot bank. Driving bravely along and a car came chug-chug-chugging up the bank. Vesta, the lovely mare, swished round before I could stop her and ran

away with me. And I didn't get her stopped until we got to Aislaby. And she was trembling. It was the first she'd seen.

Mary Liverseed, age 107
Billingham

Motoring

When I first got my motor-car in November 1936 it was mid-way through the DC numbers. That was the first registration. DC1 was still about in Middlesbrough, and we got on to XG. And my car was XG 4464, and a year after, almost a year after, I saw XG 5564 so at that time, 1936, '37, they were registering about 1,000 cars – vehicles – a year in Middlesbrough.

People say to me now that, 'motoring was different in your day. There wasn't the traffic.' There wasn't the traffic, but there weren't the roads. They forget that!

Harry Andrew, age 94
Marton

110

Motorbike Days

I know I went to work at a quarry near Tan Hill. And they were on with the road. They were laying a metalled road across from there to Tan Hill. And me and my brother went there to break stones with a hammer. You know, just until – they had to go through the three inch ring. There was this ring and if they didn't go through you had to break them up again. And we made forty pound a piece for t' month, you see, because we were on so much a cart-load. And I think that helped us a lot, like.

In fact, I bought a motorbike to get there. It wasn't a lot – two pound fifty! It was an OK Junior. It did us for a week or two and then I ran out of petrol. We pulled into Whaw village – pushed it and got into Whaw village. Got filled up with petrol and – I don't know – I think he must have spilled some petrol over the engine as he filled it. And I started it up and I got onto Whaw bridge and it burst into flames! I got off quickly and before we could do anything with it, it burned out. So that was the end of my motorbike days.

Fremont Hutchinson, age 88
Reeth

Travelling Time

One or two in the valley here were getting cars. Bill Storey had got a car, about a 1936 thing, like a hearse. And Tommy Hilton had a little 1919 Baby Austin which would be worth a lot today. And Jim Anderson had like a BSA three-wheeler. And so they were getting them – so we thought, 'By God!

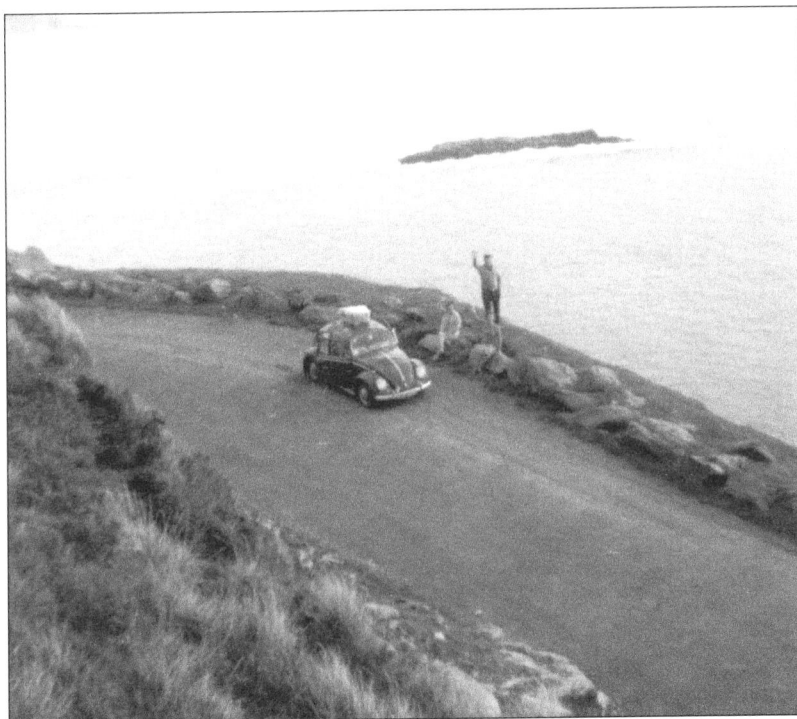

'The People's car'. Bill Wigston's VW Beetle on a touring holiday in Ireland, 1967. (Bill Wigston)

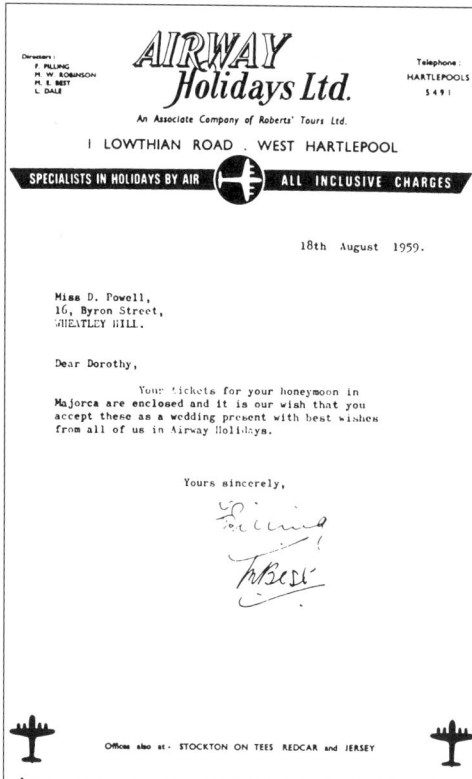

AIRWAY
Holidays Ltd.

An Associate Company of Roberts' Tours Ltd.

Directors:
F. PILLING
H. W. ROBINSON
M. E. BEST
L. DALE

Telephone:
HARTLEPOOLS
5491

1 LOWTHIAN ROAD · WEST HARTLEPOOL

SPECIALISTS IN HOLIDAYS BY AIR   ALL INCLUSIVE CHARGES

18th August 1959.

Miss D. Powell,
16, Byron Street,
WHEATLEY HILL.

Dear Dorothy,

Your tickets for your honeymoon in
Majorca are enclosed and it is our wish that you
accept these as a wedding present with best wishes
from all of us in Airway Holidays.

Yours sincerely,

Offices also at - STOCKTON ON TEES REDCAR and JERSEY

The letter to Dorothy Peacock from Mr Pilling and Miss Best, accompanying her tickets to Majorca, 1959.

We'd better get a car,' you see.

When we went from here to Gateshead, we used to set away at about half-past seven in the morning. Got the school bus that used to take us down to Toft Hill. We used to walk so far down, get another bus and then there was about a quarter of an hour's walk from where the bus dropped you in Bishop, Prince's Street, to the other end. And then the buses – a lot of them – used to change at Durham and by the time you got into Gateshead it was eleven o'clock in the morning. And then, used to set away from there at about five and used to get back in here at about half-past nine, ten o' clock at night.

And to go to Carlisle, which my father's people all lived at Carlisle, well you set away early in the morning and you got to Carlisle about six o clock at night. Now I can go to Carlisle in an hour and a half.

Bill Wigston, age 69
Hamsterley

Travel Agent

You know where the steelworks is on at Greatham now, that used to be an airport. And this chap, he was a gentleman, they called him Frank Pilling and he was Major Pilling in the war. Now this was 1953. He had this vision that after the war people would want to see the world. And he'd set up this company with…it was called Roberts Tours at Stockton. Roberts Tours at Stockton was a firm like what – we would call a travel agents now, that booked coach trips up to Wales and things like that – Butlin's holiday camp. And Mr Pilling had this insight into making holidays bigger and far away. And he was a director of Roberts Tours and he opened this office which was at Army billets on the airport.

There was Miss Best who was Mr Pilling's secretary and she was a lovely lady – you know, a lady. And this chap who did the accounts, they called him Bill Waddle, now he was made director years later. There was another girl that came from Billingham called Rita, and Sylvia and myself. And we were the ones that started the business.

And we would go – the first was the Isle of Man, flying to the Isle of Man. And on these thirty-six seater planes, we flew from Newcastle first, to the Isle of Man. And they were the first inclusive holidays – package holidays. And Bill used to sit in his office and work, like, a package out, you know. How much insurance…this is how it was done, so simple.

And the flights, I mean if you were looking back in the records, were BKS. Now, people always used to say, 'BKS, what does that stand for?' thinking it was 'British' something, but it wasn't. It was three pilots in the war, from Southend, and they set up this plane business, and it was Barnby, Keegan and Stevens. And that was the aeroplanes that first came out of Newcastle airport were known as the BKS. Now they were obviously friendly with – it must have been in the Army or whatever – with

Mr Pilling and they gave him allocations of seats on his plane. So, say to the Isle of Man there was thirty-six seats, Mr Pilling and his inclusive holidays had fifteen of them.

And from that, all these little travel agents at the time started to open up – Regent Travel at Hartlepool and places like that – and they would ring in to us to see if we had a seat. And if we had a package holiday, Mr Pilling and his secretary would go over to the Isle of Man and book the hotels. And then these package holidays came from that.

And then Jersey, oh now that was something a bit special. People started to go to Jersey for their holidays. And they would fly from Newcastle Airport to Jersey. Mr Pilling would go and get all these hotels. And of course, we

Dorothy Peacock, with husband Ray, set off for Majorca on honeymoon, 1959. Believe it or not, the buildings behind them formed Newcastle Airport! (Dorothy Peacock)

used to go free, me and Sylvia. Oh, hey – people in Wheatley Hill thought I had a job second to none, you know, going free on a holiday to Jersey. I mean, people in Wheatley Hill had never been to Blackpool, you know!

And then as time went on they got a bit further and they went to Majorca. And that was – phew! That was where I went for my honeymoon. They gave me that as my wedding present, a trip to Majorca. And I still laugh about it, we had to land at Orly Airport at Paris to refuel. We did, really! And it was on a Viking aeroplane which was much bigger than the Dakotas. I mean they could get, I think it was, fifty-four people on those!

It must have taken six or seven hours – you know, landing and then up again – six or seven hours it took us to get to Majorca.

Dorothy Peacock, age 60
Wheatley Hill

By Train

My rail stop when I was younger, when I was about four, was Peterborough. And some people will not believe me when I tell them we could leave the railway station at St John's Chapel at seven o'clock on a morning, on a steam train and I would be at Peterborough, in my gran's, lunchtime. And if you wanted to go to London, you would leave St John's Chapel at seven o'clock and at half-past twelve you were in King's Cross.

Neil Pattinson, age 57
Daddry Shield, Co. Durham

No Coal

At Middlesbrough, I told the driver, 'We're nearly out of coal.' He said, 'Oh, come on, Ron, we haven't far to go.' When we got to a little place called Redcar East we had no coal at all. We had a hundred pound of steam. That meant the driver couldn't go – we were using the steam to get the boiler filled with the injectors, for safety reasons. And he got off his stool and he give me a lecture. And I said, 'Now, look Jack,' – you understand me and Jack were the best of friends really, but this was a heated moment in our lives – I says, 'Look, Jack, if you can find any coal in that tender, I'm quite willing to put it on.' And he says, 'Ron, don't take this attitude with me,' he says, 'Come on, get some steam!'

So I says to him, 'Just have a look in there, look.' Opened the – it was like a clipper door, there's this latch. Open the latch and you can walk in the tender – well, like a bunker. And there wasn't a hap'orth of coal. And he says, 'Hey, Ron!' He says, 'We haven't got any coal! What are we going to do?' I said, 'I've been telling you this for twenty minutes!'

So we stood and the passengers are getting aggravated. The guard come down wanting to know why we weren't going. He'd been whistling his head off and we're taking no notice. And I just looked down the platform and there were two tubs of coal. I says, 'Hey! There's some coal. Come on, lads!' And we all mucked in, the guard helped as well because you had to go down a few steps to get to the coal. And we carried about twenty scuttles of coal to pump the engine up to get to the last little bit over the climb out of Redcar East and drop down into Saltburn.

And we were doing about ten mile an hour and the station inspector was running alongside: 'What's the matter, driver, what's the matter?' I said, 'well, we've no coal!' 'Come on, now,' he says, 'I've been on the railway thirty-odd years and I've never heard a driver tell me that he has no coal.' I says, 'Well, come on here and have a look.' So he went in and he had a look and he says, 'You haven't got any coal!' I says, 'Well, that's the reason why we're late!'

Ron Hick, age 72
Darlington

Part of the Holiday

I found that it was possible to get passes which would take us right through France and we started going to Italy on the train. Which was a marvellous experience, because it was part of the holiday. We used to go to London, stay overnight, get the boat train to Dover, across to Calais on the ferry and then catch the train from Calais to Gare du Nord in Paris. And, of course, that coach that we were in was transferred onto the blue train at the Gare de Lyon and they used to take us through the night down to Marseilles. Half-past seven next morning you were at Marseilles and then you had a beautiful ride all along the French Riviera to the Italian border where you had to change trains. But it was a nice break then because you could get off the train and go into the market and get strawberries and fruit, and come back and get on the Italian train. And

British Rail fireman Ron Hick, sketched on holiday, possibly at Filey, in 1948. (Ron Hick)

suddenly life seemed to take on a new dimension.

Ron Davies Evans, age 77
Darlington

Amazing Journeys

I was about eight, and I remember our teacher was Mrs Boland. I always remember, it was the first time anybody queried me and I realised by having a car you were something different. She went round the class when I was at

CWS holidays, probably Blackpool. (Norma Templeman)

Marsh Road, and she said, 'We're going to Marske. We're going to go on a bus trip.' You needed a shilling to go on it. She was going round all the lads and lasses in the class and she got to me and she said, 'Derek, you'll be going,' And I said, 'No.' And she said, 'No – you want to come with us.' And I said, 'No, Miss, I don't.' And whether or not she thought my dad and mother couldn't afford it, she said, 'It's only a shilling, Derek.' And I said, 'I don't want to go, Miss.' And she said, 'Why?' I said, 'I've been.' She said, 'You've been to Marske? How have you been to Marske?' I said, 'My dad took me in the car.'

And this is the time when, I mean, the only person who had a car in our school was our headmaster. And for one of the kids to go in, in a working-class area and to say you've got a car and you've been to somewhere…I always remember the look on her face and she sort of… 'really?'

And we used to have days out. But it wasn't just little ones. Again, it was nice journeys…vast trip up to Whitley Bay – I mean that was amazing. To go through Sunderland, and go over one river – I mean, it was bad enough to go over the Tees. I mean, once you got over the Tees, you were in Durham. That was bad enough because we're Yorkshire here. But to go across one river, and then to

116

another river – the Wear – and then go across to Newcastle and then go all along the Tyne and seeing this river and then going up the coast again…amazing thing to do, it really was.

And you'd heard songs – *The Scotswood Road*, you know, 'Whoa, me lads…' and all that, you know…we thought, 'We're going to Scotswood!' When you were coming back from Whitley Bay, or North Shields and you got to the bridge, your mam and dad would say, 'If you go that way, that's the Scotswood Road, that's the way to Scotswood.' You'd start singing the song. It was one of those mystical places. You'd only ever sang the song. You know, I suppose if you'd heard Tony Bennett, *I Left My Heart in San Francisco*, you'd want to go there!

Derek Field, age 50
Hemlington

Air Traffic Control

And then, of course, he got permission and licence to fly from Greatham Airport. Greatham Airport was only used during the war, obviously for the landing of military aircraft. And when I think about it now, Sylvia and I used to go mushrooming on the field for our dinners! We used to go out and there were sheep on the runway! I mean, the farmer on the next field used to put his sheep on in the winter because you didn't have – nobody went on their holidays in the winter, that's another thing that sticks in my mind. Our season, we worked right out from January 'til September. And then from September to January we had nothing to do. So the farmer use to put the sheep on the runway and we used to say, 'Oh, there's a plane coming in from London.' And there was a girl called

Dorothy Peacock (right) with her colleague Rita Robertson at Greatham Airport, Teesside, *c.* 1957. (Dorothy Peacock)

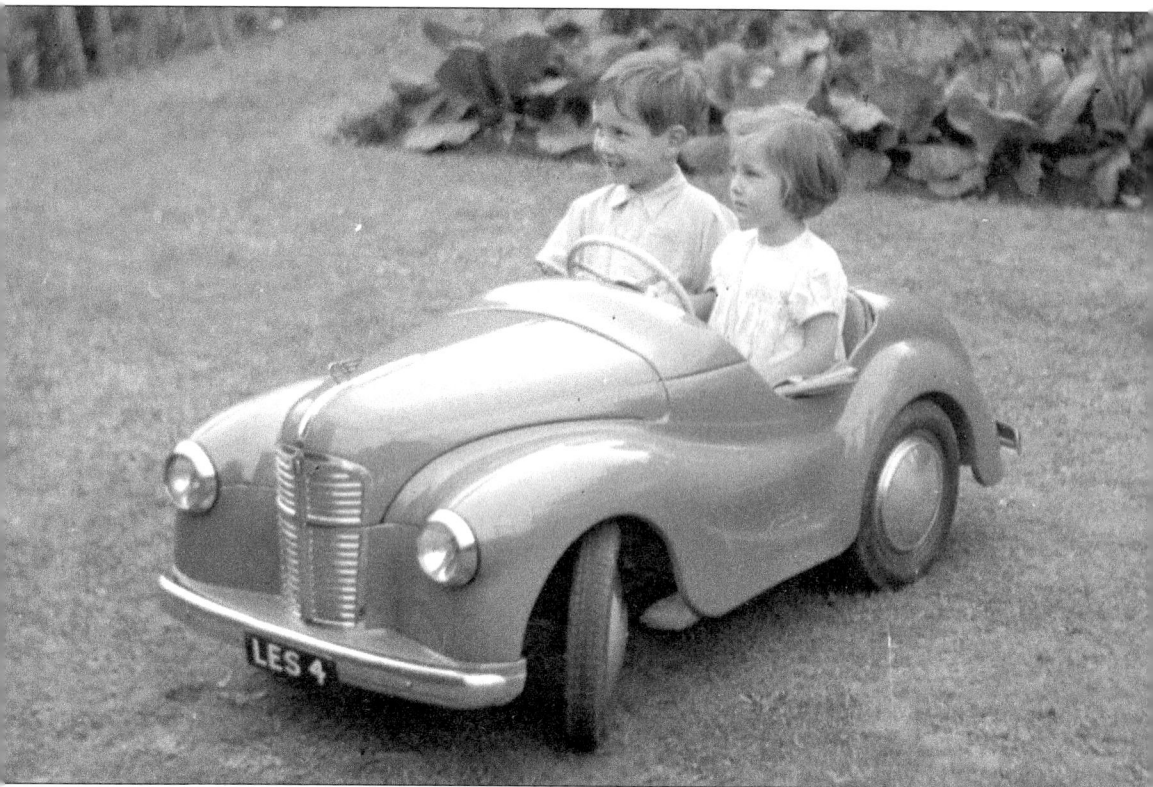

Les Clarke, aged four, August 1951. He sits in a birthday present – a specially obtained Austin pedal car, with his godmother's daughter Sylvia Smith. Note the personalised number plate! (Les Clarke)

Dorothy used to be in the tower – air traffic control. One girl – and she used to say, 'There's still some sheep out 'ere!' And the beacons, if they came in on a night, there was lighted beacons to show them where the runway was. And Herbie used to be the caretaker of the thing, and he used to go out and put these beacons on, up the runway, for this Dakota to land – a plane coming in from London.

Dorothy Peacock, age 60
Wheatley Hill

CHAPTER 11

Doing you good

Most people that we spoke to put improvements in our health and health care at the top of their lists of 'best things about the twentieth century'; and with good reason. Also, lots of interviewees think this is just the beginning – if only we can find ways of paying for the advances which medicine is sure to make.

Inside the chemist's shop on Finkle Street, Stockton on Tees. (Beamish. The North of England Open Air Museum, Co. Durham)

Seventeen Children

Well, to start, my great-grandfather, Richard Barrigan, was an Irishman. And he married Eliza Jordan, Burden or Deadon – she never seemed to be sure of her maiden name. Now, they went on to have seventeen children, one of whom obviously became my maternal grandmother.

When she had her last child – the last remaining child alive, who is now in his eighties and lives in London – she went into labour with that child on the Friday before my grandma was being married on the Saturday. And she laboured and laboured and laboured and was making no headway at all. And the doctor said to her, 'I'm sorry, Mrs Barrigan, I'm going to have to use forceps to deliver this baby.' She said,

Richard and Liza Barrigan, great-grandparents of Pat Aspinall, on their Golden Wedding, 1937. They had seventeen children. (Pat Aspinall)

'Well, you're not.' She said, 'I've had seventeen and not had forceps. Move out of the way,' she said, and she got on her hands and knees and literally delivered that child herself.

And she got out of the bed at four o'clock in the afternoon – she said, 'I've got a wedding to prepare for here.' She got out of that bed at four o'clock on that afternoon and didn't go back into it until the Monday night. And that was after delivering a child herself!

Patricia Aspinall, age 60
Crook

A Certain Condition

They didn't know anything! No, they weren't as enlightened as they are today. They didn't know a thing. If you'd said to them, you know, 'The placenta…', they'd say, 'What's that?' The afterbirth, they would call it, you see. Well, now the mothers can tell you. No, they didn't realise what was happening at all. Well, they weren't taught and their parents didn't talk about it. I mean, I know from home, from my own home, my mother wouldn't discuss anything like that; 'Shh! Don't talk about it!' and I used to do it to annoy her, of course, because by this time I was trained, and I'd say, 'She's pregnant!' 'Shh! Don't say that!' I'd say, 'What am I expected to say?' 'She's in a certain condition.' I'd say, 'she's pregnant!'

Catherine Bregazzi, age 86
Middlesbrough

Catherine Bregazzi (right) as a young midwife, Trinity Street, Stockton, 1941. The building in the background is the Maternity Home, now gone. (Catherine Bregazzi)

Granny Clarke

Actually, the woman that brought me into the world, other than my mother, helped by the other woman, was one of the local people who used to go round acting as midwives and laying people out when they were dead. She actually brought 365 youngsters into the world. Old Granny Clarke.

Walter Nunn, age 78
Shildon

Childbirth

Handywomen, that's what they were. We called them handywomen.

Wonderful. Yes, I thought they were wonderful. A lot of them did quite a lot of harm I suppose, if they interfered, but I had two on the district. And they were wonderful.

Mrs Dolan was one of them, over on the north side. And they would send for her before they sent for me. And she would know when to send for me and I knew, when Mrs Dolan sent, I was needed. Yes, they were very, very good, they really were, and should have been midwives, but they hadn't been trained, you see.

Mind you, as I said, some of them did quite a bit of harm. They used to get hold of the mothers, and I'd say, 'Don't do that, love, just leave them. Let them walk about if they want to but don't do

121

that.' They used to think, with pushing them down, it brought the baby. Which it didn't, of course. But she didn't. She never interfered. She used to know, and she'd time them and she'd watch the clock. And if, for some reason or other, she'd left it a bit late, she could deal with it, before I got there. But I was always there within minutes of the baby being born. She never interfered with anything else, you know, she would leave the placenta for me to see to.

When we first went out onto the district, there was no anaesthetics at all. But I went – when gas and air was introduced – I went and took a course in gas and air and came back on the district with this great monster. It was gas and air

Ron Davies-Evans' parents, Tom and Lucy, with his sister Olive, 1914. Olive was one of four children in the family to die in childhood. (Ron Davies-Evans)

cylinders in a great package – a case.

And you had to take it with you – well, they were going to make you take it with you and I can always remember some bright spark in the Town Hall decided that we could take it on our bikes. Well, we had a black bag on the bike in the back. And do you remember the butchers' bikes? Well, they decided we could have one of those put on the front and take this. And me, stupid that I was, I offered to cycle down Albert Road with this thing on…well, it was no good. I was falling off, really unbalanced.

So of course, they decided then that if the men wanted it they would have to come and carry it, because we couldn't carry it as well. But that was one innovation.

Then, pethidine was introduced and we were allowed to take that on the district. That was wonderful. We were given that, and of course, it helped them on in labour.

Catherine Bregazzi, age 86
Middlesbrough

Fever Hospital

We had, all together, five children in the family but I was the only one that survived. Four of my brothers and sisters died in childhood. I was old enough to remember one, Constance. We both took scarlet fever – today they call it scarletina – but then it was a bit more serious for anybody taken – and we were both admitted to the fever hospital. That was in Hundens Lane in Darlington and you were isolated, of course. You were in it for six weeks. I was discharged fit again but Constance died.

I was seven and she was five. I was most distressed because I came down one morning and my mother and father and some neighbours were crying, you see, and I didn't know what it was about. And then they told me. It had quite a big effect on me because I knew my mother had lost children before and now I was the only surviving child.

Ron Davies Evans, age 77
Darlington

Mates

Your little mates would die. One in particular, we went along to this house, a friend of my father – he took me along, and there was a little girl, Mary, was my playmate. And she wasn't there any more. And I asked where she was and they told me she'd gone to Heaven with the angels. That happened and happened often. Your mates, your little friends. Their little faces would be there no longer.

Janet Jackman, age 77
Newton Aycliffe

TB

Well, they never told me that I had TB. It was a bit like AIDS is today. People feared TB. And if you were known to have it, if you coughed they would turn away. They wouldn't use a cup that you'd used.

So anyway, my doctor said I was going to have to go away for the weekend, just for observation. So I went into the sanatorium, which was

Margo Coser (*née* Hutchinson), aged seventeen, 1948. (Margo Coser)

Brierton Hospital then. And the first meal that they brought me, the knives and forks had 'TB' on them. I said, 'I'm not going to use them. I haven't got TB.' And of course, that caused great hilarity among the staff. They just said, 'You have and you've got to use them.'

So I was in the sanatorium nine months. And there was a lady in the next room to me, when I first went in. And when I had a look in, as I passed, I saw this lady and to me, she looked like an old, old lady. She died about two days later and I found out she was twenty-eight.

The treatment was – the rooms had patio doors but they were always left open. And in fact, the snow used to come on your covers. Open to the elements. I mean, Hartlepool as well. Not Switzerland!

Margo Coser, age 68
Hartlepool

Black Herbal Salve

If anything turned poisoned, we used to have a black herbal salve. It was barbaric. You used to have a piece of cloth, put like hot candle grease onto the cloth, warm it 'til it was bubbling, then slap it onto the festering point, you know.

I mean, this wasn't just in our household, it was fairly general, you know. And with all the families being involved so much – in the pits at first,

Harry Peart (right), aged nine, in 1938, with his father and brother Gilbert. (Harry Peart)

but I think the railways, possibly, over a longer period had a bigger effect because you had the railway works where two, three – up to that point – generations of people had been there; grandfathers, fathers, sons. And anything that worked, there was no television or even radio then to spread the gospel. It spread by word of mouth and if it worked then you tried it.

Walter Nunn, age 78
Shildon

Remedies

Most families had remedies to keep away the ills and chills of winter. I mean, from carrying a walnut in your pocket to having a band of wool around your wrist. Or, as in my own instance, my mother used to send me off down to the local farm to get a jar – she used to give me a jam jar and about two pennies or a penny – and say, 'Go and get a jar of goose grease.' And I knew what was going to happen. I used to go half a mile to the farm, collect this goose fat, come back home. Mother would get it and the first thing she would do was take a huge tablespoon and give me a dollop of this fat to swallow – the most sickening, horrible stuff you could imagine. So that was to kind of lubricate my insides.

Then I would strip off and she would smear me in this goose fat. I had a vest to put on the top – so a bit like a cross-channel swimmer I was smeared in this fat and this was to stay on through the winter because I had a weak chest, I was a 'chesty' child. So the goose fat stayed on and the vest went on the top, so it was like a permanent wax jacket, if you like, that kept out the winter chills.

So most people had their chest rubbed with some kind of embrocation – some strong-smelling, irritating substance that burned your skin, so you had this glowing sensation of well-being…so it had a feeling of 'doing you good.' Most things that hurt you did you good, you know. If medicines were foul-tasting and burned your throat and had a horrible smell, they were good – they were going to do you good.

Harry Peart, age 71
Darlington

Cure-all

My father's cure-all was whiskey. If we had a pain or something, we were given a teaspoon full of whiskey. If we had a headache, some of that absorbent brown paper was dipped in whiskey, or had it strewn on it, and put on one's brow. I mean, we thought it was good for us and if we were given any sort of medicine we thought we must be a little bit better.

Mary Liverseed, age 107
Billingham

For Every Ill

My grandma on my mother's side, she had a cure for every ill. Herbs type of cures, you know. She had one for yellow jaundice. She used to call it 'saladine' and it was a yellow flower that grew about three foot high and she used to pick it, boil it and strain it. And it did truly cure people. But she used to have it

'Mrs Goolard' – Brenda Horness' grandmother Jane Heseltine, with grandfather Thomas. (Brenda Horness)

growing in her garden and she used to do various things like that, you know.

Inflammation and swelling, she used to put some – buy some – she called it 'Goolard' – from the chemist and it was only coppers. You melted it in water and it was cold, and then you put cold compresses on, you see. Well, I suppose the cold as well as whatever was in the mixture did it, because you do put cold compresses on for swelling, don't you?

And the doctor rather made a bit of fun about her. He called her 'Mrs Goolard'. But it did really bring down the swelling. But she used to sometimes override the doctor. She did with my sister with the

Staff at the Lady Eieu Cottage Hospital, Bishop Auckland, 1926. Dr Tony Ferguson's father, Dr T.E. Ferguson is on the back row, second from left. From left to right, back row: Nurse Hallam, Dr T.E. Ferguson, Nurse Knaggs, Dr V.A Wardle. Front row: Matron Melling, Dr A.C.H. McCullagh, Staff Nurse Jones, Dr T.A. McCullagh. (Tony Ferguson)

yellow jaundice. And then when the doctor came back, he says, 'Ah, that medicine's done her a lot of good.' And granny said to him, 'Aha! It wasn't your medicine that did it, it was my saladine!'

Well, I won't say he wasn't suited, but ever after that, you know, he used to say, 'Well, have you got a remedy for this one?' he took it in good part but, you know, he had to have a little dig at her.

Brenda Horness, age 75
Loftus

Grin and Bear It

The doctor, when you went into his surgery, there was either three or four big jars. One was clear, with white sediment. I believe that was a stomach bottle. There was an orangey one that I think was a cough bottle and there was a reddy one that tasted nice!

And the doctor would yank your teeth out. I mean, there was the dentist. I mean I went to the same dentist – I had false teeth, both top and bottom, by the time I was nineteen – and I went to the dentist. But if you went to the doctor, he would pull your teeth out without anaesthetic.

You were taught to grin and bear pain, you know, and you put up with it. This eye-tooth was giving me hell and I came out from the grammar school – I'd been up night after night with toothache. And when he had a look at it, he said, 'There's an abscess on it and I cannot freeze it.' So, I said, 'I want it out.'

He said, 'Can you stand it?' And I was

126

between thirteen and fourteen at the time. I said, 'Yeah, I'm desperate.' You know. And he said, 'I'll tell you what, I'll take one out on either side, and I'll freeze them,' and he says 'I'll have a go at that one.'

Whey, I'm not kidding…because they push them up, the top ones, they push them up to break the root to start with. I thought he was pushing it through the top of my head. Out it came with a little yellow bag like a pea. That was the abscess on, you know.

Walter Nunn, age 78
Shildon

Doctor's Surgery

I certainly know that the surgery attendances – we could get through a morning surgery say, pre-NHS, in about an hour and a half. But after the introduction of the NHS, within a few months of its advent, those surgeries were taking twice as long. And in the evening one might be sitting in one's surgery until seven or half-past seven at night, dealing with a huge increase.
There was no doubt there was an element of people who said, 'Well, I'll go and see the doctor and get a prescription for those aspirins, or whatever,' I believe there probably was an element of that. But on the whole, I think that people treated it with respect and didn't come demanding things.

Dr Tony Ferguson, age 77
Bishop Auckland

Streptomycin

What saved me was, streptomycin was discovered. I hadn't been in the hospital very long when it was discovered, and they put me on it. It made me semi-paralysed for about a week and I was pushed round in a wheelchair. And then, gradually, my body got used to it. And then, as the doctors got to know exactly what was wrong with you, then you had to have operations. The operations were done without anaesthetic because they found that made your TB worse – it was dangerous to have anaesthetic. But you got locals. And even if you had to have a lung taken out you were semi-aware.

Margo Coser, age 68
Hartlepool

Student nurse Joan Foster (*née* Leonard) at the Friarage Hospital, Northallerton, 1958. (Joan Foster)

A group of cadet nurses at Durham County Hospital, 1955. Standing: Muriel Grey. From left to right, middle row: Edna Short, Anne Cunningham, Joan Greenwood. Front row: Pat Aspinall, Pat Aspey, Betty Bushby. (Pat Aspinall)

A Modern Miracle

I had appendicitis, it started with these pains and it turned out to be appendicitis. And I remember going to the old Sedgefield hospital, which you did then, which was wooden sort of Army huts and so on, having an operation and being in hospital for about three weeks after the operation and being fairly ill after it, I remember – feeling absolutely dreadful. And that was a minor operation compared to the two I've had since.

Eventually angina set in and caught up with me so I had a quadruple heart bypass which put me right. It is a fantastic operation because, believe me, apart from some discomfiture when the bone's knitting together, because they saw through your chest, I never had any pain or any problems with it at all. In fact, I had the operation on the Monday afternoon and I was home having tea on the Friday.

From the minute I woke up from the operation I felt a million per cent better. I was walking the next day, I was in the gym the next day, riding on the bike, and it's brilliant. I mean you can't say anything but what a marvellous job the surgeons do. It's almost a miracle, basically. A modern miracle.

Harry Davies, age 68
Billingham